Scoop Adventures

THE BEST ICE CREAM OF THE 50 STATES

PAGE STREET
PUBLISHING CO.

Copyright © 2014 Lindsay Clendaniel

First published in 2014 by
Page Street Publishing Co.
27 Congress Street, Suite 103
Salem, MA 01970
www.pagestreetpublishing.com

Distributed by Macmillan; sales in Canada by The Canadian Manda Group; distribution in Canada by The Jaguar Book Group.

17   16   15   14   1   2   3   4   5

ISBN-13: 978-1-62414-034-1
ISBN-10: 1-62414-034-3

Library of Congress Control Number: 2013952009

Cover and book design by Page Street Publishing Co.
Photo credits on page 184

Printed and bound in China

Page Street is proud to be a member of 1% for the Planet. Members donate one percent of their sales to one or more of the over 1,500 environmental and sustainability charities across the globe who participate in this program.

Scoop Adventures

THE BEST ICE CREAM OF THE 50 STATES

Make the Real Recipes from the Greatest
Ice Cream Parlors in the Country

Lindsay Clendaniel

TOP ICE CREAM AFICIONADO
AND CREATOR OF THE BLOG SCOOPADVENTURES.COM

PAGE STREET
PUBLISHING CO.

Contents

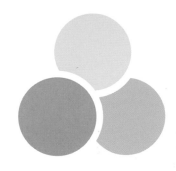

Introduction

Ice cream has always occupied a special place in my heart. Well, my stomach to be more exact. Growing up, my mother was fond of saying that ice cream always "fills in the cracks," her way of saying that she never says no to ice cream. I guess she rubbed off on me. In my world there is always an excuse for ice cream. Ice cream may be an afternoon snack, a treat enjoyed from a roadside stand, the star of a dinner party or an indulgence during a night out with friends. Sometimes there is nothing better than a quiet moment with a well-conceived scoop of vanilla bean ice cream. There are plenty of crevices and cracks in life to happily fill with ice cream.

Enjoying various scoops throughout my childhood quickly translated into a passion for all things ice cream as an adult. I began to explore the world, and I sought out every type of ice cream I could find. After eating ice cream made by other people for nearly 30 years, I decided to buy my own ice cream maker. I churned my first batch of vanilla bean ice cream the day I bought the machine, and I did not stop. With every new batch of ice cream, I set out to create a flavor that was more interesting or more intriguing than the last. My husband was a willing and eager participant in my ice cream experimentation, but soon I wanted to share my ice cream with other people, even people I did not know. And thus Scoop Adventures began.

I started writing the Scoop Adventures blog in August 2009. I was enjoying the creation of ice cream so much that I felt the need to share my discoveries with the world, to find other people with a passion for ice cream as strong, and perhaps as crazy, as mine. My first recipe for the blog was Thai Tea ice cream. I had just finished dinner at a Thai restaurant and enjoyed a cloyingly sweet glass of Thai iced tea. As I sipped the last of my beverage I realized that tea could be an interesting ice cream flavor. I set to work on the flavor that evening and posted my success for the world to see.

After my first blog post, I was hooked. Sure, my mother was the only person reading the blog, but I felt like I was embarking on a new adventure. Like many food bloggers, Scoop Adventures became a place for me to catalog recipes while sharing my love for food and flavor. Eventually, the ice cream lovers out there found me. Comments started appearing and people were making the recipes. It was fun to hear about the ice cream adventures of others. And so to please them, and my appetite, I kept churning ice cream.

My love of all things ice cream stayed with me as I celebrated many milestones. Through college, marriage, moving across country, and starting my first real job, my passion for ice cream never wavered. My experiments with ice cream continued through it all. For a few years I landed in the lively city of New Orleans. Ice cream helped me start friendships, spark conversation, and get my feet wet in the food community. Ice cream also gave me the unique opportunity to meet people from the exciting culinary world of the city. Ice cream kept me grounded and focused on a passion while the rest of life flew by. Do I ever get sick of ice cream, you ask? Well, it is a lot like other things I love—I get sick of it every once in a while, but it is not long before I figure out I cannot live without it.

Many people ask me where I find inspiration for ice cream flavors. One word—food. Food, glorious food. I love food. I am a true believer in the slow food movement, taking time to cook and enjoy food for its ability to bring people together and make people happy. Taking time to enjoy food has helped me better understand flavor and spice and seasoning. It has helped me become a better ice cream maker. I find inspiration from food in my garden, at restaurants, in my kitchen and at the grocery store. Friends and family often suggest flavors and pairings, and I love seeing the look on their faces when they taste what I have created. People and smiles give me inspiration.

As I kept churning scoops and writing blog posts, word got out about my blog and my obsession with ice cream. People started to take notice, and soon enough I was approached with a book deal. So here I sit, writing a cookbook about ice cream, still finding it hard to believe that I have been given this opportunity. Not only do I get to share some of my own favorite recipes with you, but I also get to share some of the best ice cream recipes the country has to offer. I have worked with ice cream shop owners from every region to bring you their most creative and innovative flavors. And not surprisingly, I have found other ice cream nerds getting excited about ice cream across the United States.

The ice cream parlors presented in this cookbook are not just a random group of typical scoop shops. This cookbook features a collection of recipes from shop owners who are passionate about their homemade product. They take care in selecting the best ingredients for their ice creams. The shop owners enjoy being part of their communities and have a love of making people happy through their ice cream. You will notice that their passion and creativity shine through the unique flavors they produce. They all hope that you enjoy their recipes as much as they enjoy making them.

Whether you read this cookbook from cover to cover or flip through and pick recipes at random, I believe you will find a recipe to suit every taste. Try an original homemade recipe directly from your favorite ice cream parlor, a thoughtfully adapted recipe made specifically for your home ice cream maker, or a unique flavor inspired by discussion with inventive shop owners. Start with a familiar flavor or begin with a flavor that seems completely off-the-wall. Whatever recipe you choose to embark on your ice cream journey, be sure to share your ice cream. You are certain to receive some smiles, and perhaps ice cream will become your new passion.

Love people. Make them ice cream.

THE SUGARY SOUTHEAST

Delaware, District of Columbia, Florida, Georgia, Maryland, North Carolina,
South Carolina, Virginia, West Virginia

To me, the Southeast is home. I grew up just south of the Mason-Dixon Line. Childhood summers in Maryland were filled with swim camps, mini golf and trips to the local ice cream stand. I fondly remember the excitement and indecision of choosing a flavor, then peering over the top of the counter to watch my ice cream being scooped as I waited with excited anticipation. There was nothing better than lapping up the sweet and creamy ice cream as it slid off the cone and dripped down my hand.

Although my memories are not unique to my home state, the presence of a plethora of ice cream shops in this region suggests that many children have enjoyed the same experience. The trail from north to south will take you from the sweet and salty flavor of Junk in the Tree Trunk, to the decadence of Chocolate Orange, to the fruitiness of Pink Panther and the sun-kissed flavor of Abuela Maria.

From the bayside states of Maryland and Delaware, through the historic towns of D.C., Virginia and West Virginia, along the beaches of North and South Carolina, to the rolling hills of Georgia and the blue waters of Florida, the flavors of the Southeast are as diverse as the states. Try out the recipes in this chapter to experience something unique at every turn.

Honey Sunflower Seed Ice Cream
Moorenko's, Silver Spring, Maryland

MAKES 1 GENEROUS QUART (940ML)

Honey Sunflower Seed is one of owner Susan Soorenko's favorite flavors from her shop because it is a wonderful sweet and salty change from the ubiquitous Salted Caramel. This ice cream embodies the same sweet and savory appeal of caramel ice cream but is a bit edgier. The toasted sunflower seeds pair beautifully with the bold flavor of the wildflower honey. Serve with your favorite fresh fruit.

TOASTED SUNFLOWER SEEDS

1 tbsp (15ml) fruity olive oil

¾ cup (120g) raw sunflower seeds

1 ½ tsp sea salt

ICE CREAM BASE

½ cup (118ml) wildflower honey (or dark honey of choice)

2 cups (473ml) heavy cream

5 large egg yolks

1 cup (237ml) whole milk

¼ cup (50g) sugar

Pinch of salt

To prepare the sunflower seeds, coat a heavy skillet with olive oil, removing the excess. Add the sunflower seeds and stir to lightly coat. Sprinkle salt over the seeds and toast over medium heat, stirring occasionally, until the seeds start to brown and become fragrant, about 5 minutes. Once toasted, let the sunflower seeds sit in the pan for a few minutes, then refrigerate to cool completely before adding to the ice cream.

To make the ice cream base, warm the honey slightly. Pour the cream into a medium bowl and mix in the warmed honey. Set aside. Whisk the egg yolks in a medium bowl and set aside. Combine the milk, sugar and pinch of salt in a medium saucepan. Warm over medium heat until the mixture is hot and the sugar is dissolved, 4 to 5 minutes. Temper the eggs by slowly pouring ½ cup (120ml) of the warmed milk mixture into the yolks, whisking constantly until combined. Return the warmed yolks to the pan with the remaining milk mixture. Heat the custard over medium-low heat, stirring constantly, until the custard thickens and coats the back of a spoon. Remove from the heat and pour through a fine-mesh sieve into the bowl with the cream and honey mixture. Cool to room temperature. Cover and refrigerate until well chilled, at least 4 hours or overnight.

Once chilled, pour the base into your ice cream maker and churn according to the manufacturer's instructions. Just before the ice cream is finished churning, add the toasted sunflower seeds (save a few seeds to sprinkle on top of the finished ice cream). Transfer to a freezer-safe container and sprinkle with the remaining sunflower seeds. Freeze until firm, at least 4 hours. Serve soft over fresh summer fruit or keep in your freezer to eat standing up in the middle of the night.

UDairy Creamery
from the cow to the cone

Junk in the Tree Trunk Ice Cream

Adapted from recipe by UDairy Creamery, University of Delaware, Newark, Delaware

MAKES 1½ QUARTS (1.4L)

I have a sweet spot in my heart for this flavor because it is made by my alma mater. The UDairy Creamery did not open until after I graduated college; however, it is hard to resist a sweet and gooey maple ice cream produced with milk from cows that roam near campus. This flavor was inspired by the botanical gardens at the University of Delaware's College of Agriculture & Natural Resources, close to where they make the ice cream.

ICE CREAM BASE

2 cups (473ml) heavy cream

1 ½ cups (355ml) whole milk

¼ cup (50g) sugar

¾ tsp vanilla extract

¾ cup (177ml) dark maple syrup

PRALINE

¾ cup (151g) packed brown sugar

⅓ cup (79ml) half-and-half

1 tbsp (14g) butter

¼ cup (33g) confectioners' sugar

1 cup (120g) chopped pecans

½ cup (118ml) caramel topping (store-bought or page 52)

To make the ice cream base, fill a large bowl with ice water and set aside. Combine the cream, milk, sugar, vanilla and maple syrup in a medium saucepan. Place over medium heat and warm until the mixture is hot and the sugar and maple syrup are dissolved, 4 to 5 minutes. Remove from the heat and transfer to a medium bowl. Set the bowl in the ice water bath to cool, 20 minutes, whisking occasionally. Cover and refrigerate until well chilled, at least 4 hours or overnight.

While the ice cream base is cooling, make the praline. Combine the brown sugar, half-and-half, butter and confectioners' sugar in a medium saucepan. Warm the ingredients over medium heat, stirring constantly, until the mixture bubbles and begins to rise. Remove the saucepan from the heat and add the pecans. Stir until the pecans are evenly coated, then pour into a shallow container. Freeze until cool and ready to use. The mixture will not completely harden.

Once the ice cream base is chilled, pour the base into an ice cream maker and churn according to the manufacturer's instructions. Break up the praline into smaller pieces (this process will be messy). When churning is complete, gently fold in the praline pieces and the caramel topping. Transfer to a freezer-safe container and freeze until firm, at least 4 hours. The longer you allow the praline to sit in the ice cream, the gooier it will become.

Blueberry Kale Ice Cream
The Hop Ice Cream Café, Asheville, North Carolina

MAKES ABOUT 1 QUART (940ML)

I know what you're thinking. Kale in ice cream? Thankfully, the owners of The Hop decided to give it a shot. After all, adding spinach, kale and other super greens to smoothies and juices is already a national health trend, so it made sense to create a "green" ice cream. To make the ice cream more accessible to the public, a sweet blueberry swirl was added using local berries when available. Besides moonlighting as a healthier twist on ice cream, this flavor is an especially tasty and attractive scoop. Give it a try—you will be pleasantly surprised.

ICE CREAM BASE

5 egg yolks

¾ cup (150g) + 3 ½ tsp (42g) sugar, divided

2 cups (473ml) heavy cream

¾ cup (177ml) milk

Pinch of salt

2 oz (56g) raw kale, torn into small pieces

2 ½ tsp (12ml) lemon juice

½ tsp lemon zest

BLUEBERRY SWIRL

½ cup (96g) fresh blueberries

4 tsp (16g) sugar

To make the ice cream base, whisk the egg yolks and ¼ cup (50g) of the sugar in a medium bowl until pale in color; set aside. In a medium saucepan, combine the cream, milk, ½ cup (100g) sugar and a pinch of salt. Place the pan over medium heat and warm until the mixture is hot and the sugar dissolves, 3 to 4 minutes. Temper the eggs by slowly pouring ½ cup (120ml) of the warmed cream mixture into the yolks, whisking constantly until combined. Return the warmed yolks to the pan with the remaining cream mixture. Heat the custard over medium-low heat, stirring constantly, until the custard thickens and coats the back of a spoon. Remove from the heat and pour through a fine-mesh sieve into a medium bowl. Cool to room temperature. Cover and refrigerate until well chilled, at least 4 hours or overnight.

Once the custard is chilled, combine 1 cup (237ml) of the cooled custard, the kale, the remaining 3 ½ teaspoons (42g) sugar, lemon juice and lemon zest in a blender. Purée until smooth. Combine with the remaining custard, taste and add more lemon juice if desired. Pour the ice cream base into an ice cream machine and churn according to the manufacturer's instructions.

While the ice cream is churning, make the blueberry swirl. Purée the blueberries and sugar in a food processor or blender. Once churning is complete, transfer the ice cream to a freezer-safe container and gently swirl in the blueberry purée, evenly distributing but leaving a thick ribbon of purée. Freeze overnight.

Tip: For added sweetness, mix half of the blueberry swirl into the ice cream base before churning, and then fold in the remaining swirl once the ice cream is churned.

Pink Panther Ice Cream

Adapted from recipe by Ellen's Homemade Ice Cream, Charleston, West Virginia

MAKES 1 QUART (940ML)

In addition to being an ice cream maker, owner Ellen Beal performs as a flutist with the West Virginia Symphony. She was inspired to create this flavor during a Pops concert in which the symphony performed music from the Pink Panther movie. While speaking to the audience, the conductor indicated he thought pink panther sounded like it should be an ice cream flavor! The audience seemed to like the suggestion, so Ellen set to work in her shop, creating a fruity and tart ice cream using the cocktail of the same name as inspiration.

6 oz (170g) fresh raspberries

1 tbsp (15ml) orange juice concentrate

1 ¾ cups (414ml) heavy cream

1 ¼ cups (295ml) whole milk

¾ cup (150g) sugar

Pinch of salt

1 tsp orange zest

2 ½ tbsp (37ml) crème de cassis

Place the raspberries in a blender and purée until smooth. Strain the purée through a fine-mesh sieve to remove the seeds. In a medium bowl, combine the raspberry purée with the orange juice concentrate. Cover and set aside.

Combine the cream, milk, sugar, salt and orange zest in a medium saucepan. Place over medium heat and bring the milk mixture to a low boil. Cook until the sugar dissolves, 3 minutes. Remove from the heat and pour through a sieve into the raspberry–orange juice mixture. Cool to room temperature. Once cool, stir in the cassis. Cover and refrigerate until well chilled, at least 4 hours or overnight.

Once chilled, pour the ice cream base into an ice cream maker and churn according to the manufacturer's instructions. Transfer to a freezer-safe container and freeze until firm, at least 4 hours.

Lemon Ricotta Cardamom Gelato
Adapted from recipe by Dolcezza, Washington, D.C.

MAKES 1 QUART (940ML)

Owner Robb Duncan was approached one Sunday afternoon by a fellow farmers' market vendor, who offered to provide him with fresh ricotta cheese to use in his gelato. Soon a food partnership was born. Robb began making Honey Ricotta Gelato and then Almond Ricotta, but he still felt something was missing. When he changed his recipe to Lemon Ricotta Cardamom, the flavor was an instant winner with the folks at the farmers' market and now in his four shops. The gelato has a lovely balance of playful ricotta in the base, lemon riding on top with acidity and brightness, and cardamom to bring out the flavors.

LEMON SYRUP

2 to 3 lemons

2 tbsp (25g) sugar

GELATO BASE

2 ½ cups (592ml) whole milk

½ cup (118ml) heavy cream

⅔ cup (133g) sugar

¼ cup (59ml) corn syrup

½ cup (118ml) whole milk ricotta cheese

Pinch of salt

¼ to ½ tsp ground cardamom

To prepare lemon syrup, use a vegetable peeler to remove the zest of one lemon in large strips; set aside. Squeeze the lemons until you have 6 tablespoons (90ml) of juice. Combine the juice with the sugar in a small saucepan and place over medium heat. Heat until the sugar is dissolved, 1 to 2 minutes. Pour into a small bowl, cover and refrigerate until completely cool.

To prepare the base, combine the milk, cream, sugar, corn syrup and reserved lemon zest in a medium saucepan and place over medium heat. Warm the base until bubbles begin to form, stirring occasionally to combine the ingredients. Remove from the heat and transfer to a medium bowl. Allow to cool for 5 minutes, and then add the ricotta and salt, whisking to combine. Cover and chill the base in the refrigerator for at least 4 hours or overnight.

When ready to churn, remove the lemon zest. Add the lemon syrup to the chilled gelato base and whisk to combine. Add the cardamom. Taste and add more cardamom if needed (you should taste light floral aromatic notes from middle to end). Once you are pleased with the taste, pour the gelato base into an ice cream maker and churn according to the manufacturer's instructions. Churn until the gelato has reached the consistency of a barely pourable smoothie. Transfer to a freezer-safe container and freeze until firm, at least 4 hours.

Tips: Buy the freshest and best ricotta cheese you can find. Do not squeeze lemons until the last minute to have the freshest lemon juice possible. Be careful with the cardamom, because it can be very unforgiving.

Orange Chocolate Decadence
Adapted from recipe by Bev's Homemade Ice Cream, Richmond, Virginia

MAKES 1 GENEROUS QUART (940ML)

Orange and chocolate are a winning combination. If you have never tried these flavors together, now is the time to start. Acidic and sweet orange is the perfect complement to the creamy and thick chocolate base in this ice cream. A touch of vanilla brings out the floral quality of the orange. After you try this scoop, you may never go back to plain chocolate.

CHOCOLATE LIQUOR

½ cup (56g) cocoa powder

¼ cup (59ml) water

⅓ cup (67g) sugar

ICE CREAM BASE

3 egg yolks

1 orange

2 cups (473ml) heavy cream, divided

1 ½ cups (355ml) whole milk

½ cup (100g) sugar

Pinch of salt

½ tsp vanilla extract

2 tsp (10ml) orange liqueur (optional)

To make the chocolate liquor, combine the cocoa powder, water and sugar in a small saucepan. Place the saucepan over low heat and bring to a low boil, whisking constantly until the ingredients are combined. Remove from the heat, pour into a medium bowl and set aside.

To make the ice cream base, fill a large bowl with ice water. Whisk the egg yolks in a medium bowl and set aside. Use a vegetable peeler to remove the zest of the orange in large strips and set aside. Squeeze the orange and pour the juice into a small saucepan. Bring to a boil, reduce the heat and simmer until the juice is half its original volume, 4 minutes. Remove from the heat and set aside.

In a medium saucepan, combine ¾ cup (177ml) of the cream, milk, sugar, reserved orange zest and pinch of salt. Place the pan over medium heat and warm until the mixture is hot and the sugar dissolves, 4 to 5 minutes. Temper the eggs by slowly pouring ½ cup (120ml) of the warmed cream mixture into the yolks, whisking constantly until combined. Return the warmed yolks to the pan with the remaining cream mixture. Heat the custard over medium-low heat, stirring constantly, until the custard thickens and coats the back of a spoon. Remove from the heat and pour through a fine-mesh sieve into the bowl with the chocolate liquor. Remove the zest from the sieve and return it to the ice cream base. Add the reserved orange juice and remaining 1 ¼ cups (295ml) cream and stir to combine. Set the bowl in the ice water bath to cool, 20 minutes, whisking occasionally. Add the vanilla and stir to combine. Cover and refrigerate until well chilled, at least 4 hours or overnight.

Once chilled, remove the zest from the ice cream base. Add the orange liquor, if using. Pour the base into an ice cream machine and churn according to the manufacturer's instructions. Transfer to a freezer-safe container and freeze for at least 4 hours.

Balsamic Fig Ice Cream
Adapted from recipe by High Road Craft Ice Cream & Sorbet, Atlanta, Georgia

MAKES 1½ QUARTS (1.4L)

Atlanta is a city known for its heat, but the cold sweeps through for a bit every winter. For the owners of High Road Craft, the cold weather often sparks cravings for dried figs. Pairing sweet figs with savory and tart balsamic vinegar helps bring a beautiful balance to this dessert, making it less cloyingly sweet and a more intriguing flavor. Serve as an elegant ice cream paired with olive oil or butter-toasted pound cake.

BALSAMIC GLAZE

¾ cup (177ml) balsamic vinegar

¼ tsp honey

Pinch of salt

ICE CREAM BASE

¾ cup (124g) dried figs, stems removed

1 ½ cups (355ml) water

¾ tsp lemon zest

¼ tsp kosher salt

6 egg yolks

1 ½ cups (355ml) heavy cream

1 ½ cups (355ml) skim milk

1 cup (237ml) sweetened condensed milk

¾ cup (150g) sugar

To prepare balsamic glaze, pour the vinegar into a small saucepan and place over medium-high heat. Bring to a boil, reduce the heat and simmer until syrupy, about 12 minutes. Remove from the heat and stir in the honey and salt. Cool completely before adding to the ice cream.

To make the ice cream base, place the figs and water in a small saucepan and bring to a rolling boil. Remove from the heat, cover and let stand at room temperature for 30 minutes. Drain the figs, reserving 3 tablespoons (45ml) of the fig-steeped hot water. Combine the figs, reserved water, lemon zest and salt in a food processor and purée until smooth. Set aside.

Fill a large bowl with ice water; set aside. Whisk the egg yolks in a medium bowl and set aside. Combine the cream, milk, condensed milk and sugar in a medium saucepan. Place over medium heat and bring to a simmer. Temper the eggs by slowly pouring 1 cup (237ml) of the warmed cream mixture into the yolks, whisking constantly until combined. Return the warmed yolks to the pan with the remaining cream mixture. Heat the custard over low heat, stirring constantly, until the custard thickens and coats the back of a spoon, 2 minutes. Remove from the heat and pour through a fine-mesh sieve into a medium bowl. Set the bowl in the ice water bath to cool, 20 minutes, whisking occasionally. Add the fig mixture and whisk to combine. Cover and refrigerate until well chilled, at least 4 hours or overnight.

Once chilled, pour the ice cream base into an ice cream maker and churn according to the manufacturer's instructions. When churning is complete, gently fold in 3 tablespoons (45ml) balsamic glaze. Transfer to a freezer-safe container and freeze until firm, at least 4 hours. Serve with more balsamic glaze and fresh figs.

Chunky Turtle Ice Cream
Inspired by Wholly Cow Ice Cream, Charleston, South Carolina

MAKES 1 QUART (940ML)

Caramelized and almost burnt is one of the best ways to eat sugar. Caramel has been a favorite in candies and chocolates for a long time, but more recently ice cream shop owners have discovered the goodness of using caramel to flavor ice cream. Salted caramel is one of the most popular flavors in ice cream shops today. Wholly Cow adds glorious South Carolina pecans and chunks of chocolate to their version of caramel ice cream, resulting in a sweet, salty, crunchy, chocolate-filled scoop.

ICE CREAM BASE

1 ½ cups (355ml) whole milk, divided

1 tbsp (9g) cornstarch

⅔ cup (133g) sugar

1 ¾ cups (414ml) heavy cream

½ tsp salt

¾ cup (128g) salted pecans (see below)

2 oz (56g) dark chocolate, finely chopped

SALTED PECANS

¾ cup (128g) unsalted pecan pieces

1 tbsp (14g) unsalted butter, melted

½ tsp salt

To make the ice cream base, fill a large bowl with ice water. In a small bowl, combine 2 tablespoons (30ml) of the milk with the cornstarch, whisk and set aside. Measure the sugar into a large, deep saucepan and place over medium heat. Do not touch the sugar until all edges begin to melt, then cook the sugar until it begins to brown, stirring gently and frequently, allowing the sugar to reach a deep amber color. Immediately and carefully add about ¼ cup (60ml) of the cream. Be careful: The mixture will bubble and spit when adding cream to the hot sugar; the sugar will harden but when returned to heat will melt again. Add remaining cream until complete, stirring to combine.

Return the pan to medium heat. Add the remaining milk and bring the mixture to a boil. Cook for 3 minutes, or until all caramelized sugar dissolves. Remove from the heat and gradually whisk in the cornstarch mixture. Return to a boil and cook over moderately high heat until the mixture is slightly thickened, about 1 minute. Pour into a medium bowl. Whisk in the salt. Set the bowl in the ice water bath to cool, 20 minutes, whisking occasionally. Cover and refrigerate until well chilled, at least 4 hours or overnight.

To make the salted pecans, preheat the oven to 350°F (180°C, or gas mark 4). Combine all the ingredients in a medium bowl, tossing to coat the pecans. Spread the mixture evenly on a baking sheet and bake for 10 to 15 minutes, stirring once, until slightly toasted and aromatic. Let cool completely before adding to the ice cream.

Once the ice cream base is chilled, pour it into an ice cream maker and churn according to the manufacturer's instructions. When churning is complete, gently fold in the salted pecans and chocolate pieces. Transfer to a freezer-safe container and freeze until firm, at least 4 hours.

Abuela Maria Ice Cream
Azucar Ice Cream Company, Miami, Florida

MAKES 1 QUART (940ML)

Located in the heart of Little Havana, Azucar caters to the taste of customers who live near their shop. This flavor was inspired by a traditional Cuban treat featuring Maria crackers lined with a thin slice of guava paste and cream cheese. Sweet cream ice cream is the perfect accompaniment to the guava, cream cheese, and cookies in the frozen version of this delectable Cuban treat.

2 eggs

½ cup (100g) sugar

1 cup (237ml) whole milk

2 cups (473ml) heavy cream

2 tsp (10ml) vanilla extract

4 oz (113g) guava paste

3 ½ oz (99g) sleeve of Maria crackers

3 oz (57g) regular cream cheese

½ cup (118ml) guava jam or marmalade

Whisk the eggs and sugar in a medium bowl until pale in color; set aside. Pour the milk into a medium saucepan and set over medium heat, warming until the milk is hot and bubbles begin to form. Temper the eggs by slowly pouring ½ cup (120ml) of the warmed milk into the eggs, whisking constantly until combined. Return the warmed eggs to the pan with the remaining milk. Heat the custard over medium-low heat, stirring constantly, until the custard thickens and coats the back of a spoon. Remove from the heat and pour through a fine-mesh sieve into a medium bowl. Add the cream and vanilla. Cool to room temperature. Cover and refrigerate until well chilled, at least 4 hours or overnight.

When the base is thoroughly chilled, pour into an ice cream maker and churn according to the manufacturer's instructions. While the ice cream is churning, cut the guava paste into tiny cubes, break the crackers into small bite-size pieces, and cut the cream cheese into small pieces. When the ice cream has finished churning, gently fold in the pieces of guava paste and crackers. Spoon a small layer of guava marmalade and cream cheese pieces into a freezer-safe container and lightly spoon a layer of ice cream on top. Continue to alternate layers of marmalade, cream cheese and ice cream until the container is full, gently swirling with a spoon. Top with guava marmalade. Freeze until firm, at least 4 hours.

THE SWEET SOUTH

Alabama, Arkansas, Kentucky, Louisiana, Mississippi, Oklahoma, Tennessee, Texas

The South has a special place in my heart. For several years I lived in the energetic city of New Orleans. During my days in the South, I discovered that aside from their uniqueness, people of the South have passion. They are passionate about their cities, their states, their families and their food. And without exception, Southerners have a passion for ice cream.

Ice cream in the South is most influenced by the passion for food. Like those in many other regions of the United States, Southerners take pride in knowing where their food comes from and showcasing it to the world. With flavors like Steen's Molasses Oatmeal Cookie from Louisiana, Bourbon Ball from Kentucky, and Peach Honey Habanero from Texas, the South shows off its love for food in its flavors of ice cream.

Several images come to mind when I think of the South—bright lights and parties, hurricanes, music, cowboy hats, crawfish, twang and porch sitting in the summer. The South is eclectic. The South is its own character. The South has some sweet ice cream. Give these recipes a try and feel the passion of the South.

Lavender Caramel Swirl Ice Cream
Loblolly Creamery, Little Rock, Arkansas

MAKES 1 GENEROUS QUART (940ML)

Southern desserts like peach cobbler, pecan tassies and lemon chess pie are very dear to the folks at Loblolly Creamery. These sweet treats bring the owners, Sally and Rachel, back to summer days at Grandma's house, eating slices of her Southern caramel cake. So rich and decadent, the cake is a family favorite that elevates any special occasion. Made with the same decadence as Southern caramel icing with an added flare of Arkansas-grown lavender buds, this ice cream combines delicate floral notes and rich caramel to make a Southern dessert in a scoop. It is a labor of love the owners hope y'all enjoy!

ICE CREAM BASE

1 tbsp + 1 tsp (6g) dried lavender buds

⅔ cup (133g) granulated sugar

⅓ cup (67g) packed dark brown sugar

¼ tsp fine sea salt

1 tbsp + 1 tsp (20ml) wildflower honey

2 cups (474ml) whole milk

2 cups (474ml) heavy cream

CARAMEL SWIRL

⅓ cup (67g) sugar

⅓ cup (79ml) heavy cream

To make the ice cream base, combine the lavender buds, granulated sugar, dark brown sugar, salt, honey and whole milk in a medium saucepan. Cook over medium heat until hot and steam beginsπ to rise, 3 to 4 minutes. Remove from the heat, cover and steep for 15 minutes. Strain the mixture through a sieve, pressing on the lavender buds with the back of a spoon to extract flavor. Stir in the heavy cream. Cover and refrigerate overnight.

To make the caramel swirl, place the sugar in a heavy-bottomed pot over medium heat. Do not touch the sugar until all edges begin to melt, then cook the sugar until it begins to brown, stirring gently and frequently, allowing the sugar to reach a deep amber color. Remove from the heat and carefully add the heavy cream, allowing the mixture to bubble and froth without stirring. Once the caramel has ceased bubbling, cook over medium-low heat until all the sugar is dissolved. Pour into a medium bowl and cool to room temperature. Refrigerate to chill completely, preferably overnight.

When the base is thoroughly chilled, pour into an ice cream maker and churn according to the manufacturer's instructions. Place a layer of caramel in the bottom of a freezer-safe container and lightly spoon a layer of ice cream on top. Continue to alternate layers of caramel and ice cream until the container is full, gently swirling with a spoon. Top with a swirl of caramel. Freeze until firm, at least 4 hours.

Peach Honey Habanero Ice Cream
Inspired by Amy's Ice Creams, Austin, Texas

MAKES 1½ QUARTS (1.4L)

Juicy Texas peaches, sweet honey and spicy habanero are used to make this scoop at Austin's most eclectic ice cream shop. "Keep Austin Weird" is the unofficial motto of the city, and although the sweet and spicy concept for this ice cream is not too off-the-wall, the flavor is out of this world. The cool cream and sweet honey balance out the peppery kick in a scoop that provides big flavor worthy of Texas.

1 habanero pepper

½ cup (118ml) honey

1 ½ lb (680g) peaches (4 or 5 medium)

½ cup (118ml) water

½ cup (100g) sugar

2 egg yolks

1 ½ cups (355ml) heavy cream

¼ tsp lemon juice

¼ tsp vanilla extract

Pinch of salt

Preheat the oven to broil. Cut the habanero pepper in half and remove the stem and seeds. Place on a parchment- or silicone-lined baking sheet, skin side up. Roast under the broiler until charred, about 5 minutes. Remove from the oven and place in a blender with the honey. Blend until well combined. Pour into a small container and chill in the refrigerator overnight, or up to 48 hours, depending on the heat level you desire.

Peel, pit and slice the peaches. Combine the prepared peaches, water and sugar in a medium saucepan and place over medium heat. Bring to a low boil, reduce the heat and simmer until the peaches are soft, 10 to 15 minutes. Remove from the heat and cool completely. Chill in the refrigerator until ready to use in the ice cream.

Whisk the egg yolks in a medium bowl and set aside. Pour the cream into a small saucepan and heat over medium heat until the cream begins to bubble. Temper the eggs by slowly pouring ½ cup (118ml) warmed cream into the yolks, whisking constantly until combined. Return the warmed yolks to the pan with the remaining cream. Heat the custard over medium-low heat, stirring constantly, until the custard thickens and coats the back of a spoon. Remove from the heat and pour through a fine-mesh sieve into a medium bowl. Cool to room temperature. Cover and refrigerate until well chilled, at least 4 hours or overnight.

Once the base is chilled, combine the habanero honey, peaches, prepared ice cream base, lemon juice, vanilla and salt in a blender. Purée until well blended. Pour directly into an ice cream maker and churn according to the manufacturer's instructions. Transfer to a freezer-safe container and freeze for at least 4 hours.

Steen's Molasses Oatmeal Cookie Ice Cream

Creole Creamery, New Orleans, Louisiana

MAKES 1½ QUARTS (1.4L)

New Orleans is a city full of character in both its people and its food. Chefs in the area enjoy incorporating regional flavors into their cuisine, including the ice cream chefs in town. Bryan Gilmore from Creole Creamery adds sweet and syrupy Steen's molasses to this ice cream recipe, made from locally produced cane sugar, to provide a strong flavor unique to the South.

½ cup (100g) sugar

6 egg yolks

3 cups (710ml) half-and-half

1 cup (237ml) heavy cream

½ tsp ground cinnamon

½ tsp ground nutmeg

¼ cup (59ml) Steen's molasses (preferred, may substitute blackstrap molasses)

½ cup (76g) raisins

1 cup (150g) crushed oatmeal cookies

Combine the sugar and egg yolks in a small bowl and whisk until combined. Set aside. Combine the half-and-half, cream, cinnamon and nutmeg in a medium saucepan and warm over medium heat until the mixture is hot and the sugar dissolves, 4 to 5 minutes. Temper the eggs by slowly pouring the warmed cream mixture into the yolks, whisking constantly until combined. Return the mixture to the pan. Add the molasses. Heat the custard over medium-low heat, stirring constantly, until the custard thickens and coats the back of a spoon, 8 minutes. Remove from the heat and pour through a fine-mesh sieve into a medium bowl. Cool to room temperature. Cover and refrigerate until well chilled, at least 4 hours or overnight.

Once chilled, pour the ice cream base into an ice cream maker and churn according to the manufacturer's instructions. When churning is complete, gently fold in the raisins and cookie pieces. Transfer to a freezer-safe container and freeze until firm, at least 4 hours.

Mississippi Mary's Pound Cake Ice Cream

Sweet Magnolia Ice Cream Company, Clarksdale, Mississippi

MAKES 1 GENEROUS QUART (940ML)

Mrs. Mary is a family friend of Sweet Magnolia's owner, Hugh Balthrop. She has been making cakes and pies for his family for many years. According to Hugh, Mrs. Mary makes the best lemon-glazed pound cake in the state of Mississippi. A couple of years ago, Hugh decided to mix Mrs. Mary's pound cake into his French vanilla custard and it became one of his top sellers! He affectionately named the ice cream after Mrs. Mary and her famous cake, and now everyone else loves Mrs. Mary's pound cake as much as his family.

4 eggs yolks

¾ cup (150g) sugar

2 cups (473ml) whole milk

1 cup (237ml) heavy cream

1 vanilla bean

1 cup (230g) cubed pound cake, chilled (preferably lemon)*

Fill a large bowl with ice water. Whisk the egg yolks and sugar in a medium bowl until pale in color; set aside. Combine the milk and cream in a medium saucepan. Cut open the vanilla bean and scrape the vanilla seeds into the milk mixture, adding the pod as well. Set over medium heat and warm until bubbles begin to form. Temper the eggs by slowly pouring ½ cup (118ml) of the warmed milk mixture into the yolks, whisking constantly until combined. Return the warmed yolks to the pan with the remaining milk mixture. Heat the custard over medium-low heat, stirring constantly, until the custard thickens and coats the back of a spoon. Remove from the heat and pour through a fine-mesh sieve into a medium bowl. Set the bowl in the ice water bath to cool, 20 minutes, whisking occasionally. Cover and refrigerate until well chilled, at least 4 hours or overnight.

Once chilled, pour the ice cream base into an ice cream maker and churn according to the manufacturer's instructions. When churning is complete, gently fold in the pieces of pound cake. Transfer to a freezer-safe container and freeze until firm, at least 4 hours.

* If you cannot find lemon pound cake, buy regular pound cake and add lemon flavor. Make a lemon syrup by juicing three or four lemons (½ cup [118 ml] lemon juice), and combine the juice with 2 tablespoons (25g) sugar in a small saucepan. Heat until the sugar is dissolved, remove from the heat and cool completely. Pour over your pound cake about 3 to 4 hours prior to mixing it into the ice cream.

Buttermilk Honey Ice Cream
Loblolly Creamery, Little Rock, Arkansas

MAKES 1 QUART (940ML)

A simple yet versatile flavor, Buttermilk Honey Ice Cream was the first flavor ever made by Loblolly Creamery. It was developed for the Arkansas Cornbread Festival in 2011 and sat atop their caramel cornbread. The audience went gaga over the dessert, and a classic flavor was born. Serve as a sweet and tangy accompaniment to any pie or cobbler or as a beautiful pairing to a simple bowl of fruit.

¾ cup (150g) sugar

2 ½ tbsp (37ml) wildflower honey

¼ tsp fine sea salt

1 ¾ cups (414ml) heavy cream, divided

1 ¾ cups (414ml) buttermilk

Combine the sugar, honey, salt and 1 cup (237ml) of the cream in a medium saucepan. Cook over medium-low heat until all the solids are dissolved, 4 to 5 minutes. Remove from the heat and stir in the remaining ¾ cup (177ml) cream and the buttermilk. Pour into a medium bowl, cover and refrigerate until well chilled, at least 4 hours or overnight.

Once chilled, pour into an ice cream maker and churn according to the manufacturer's instructions. Transfer to a freezer-safe container and freeze for at least 4 hours.

Strawberries & Cream Ice Cream
Roxy's Ice Cream Social, Oklahoma City, Oklahoma

MAKES 1½ QUARTS (1.4L)

Roxy's Ice Cream Social is not your typical ice cream shop. It is Oklahoma City's premier gourmet hand-dipped ice cream *truck*. Named after the owner's spunky and energetic Great Dane, Roxy's is in the business of revamping the image of the ice cream truck. Strawberries & Cream is the owner's favorite flavor because it reminds her of growing up eating garden-ripe strawberries from her backyard. This recipe is different from other strawberry ice creams because it swirls the tart flavor of strawberries with the sweet creamy taste of ice cream. May it take you back to sweet memories, too.

SWEET CREAM BASE

¾ cup (177ml) whole milk, divided

2 tsp (6g) tapioca starch

1 cup (237ml) heavy cream

¼ cup (50g) sugar

2 tbsp (30ml) golden cane syrup

⅛ tsp salt

STRAWBERRY SORBET BASE

1 lb (454g) strawberries, hulled

1 cup (200g) sugar

1 cup (237ml) strawberry preserves

1 cup (237ml) water

To make the sweet cream base, whisk ¼ cup (59ml) of the milk and the tapioca starch in a small bowl and set aside. Combine the remaining ½ cup (118ml) milk, cream, sugar and cane syrup in a medium saucepan and place over medium heat. Bring the milk mixture to a low boil. Cook until the sugar dissolves, 3 minutes. Remove the milk mixture from the heat and gradually whisk in the tapioca starch mixture. Return to a boil and cook over moderately high heat until the mixture is slightly thickened, about 1 minute. Pour into a medium bowl. Whisk in the salt. Cool to room temperature. Cover and refrigerate until well chilled, at least 4 hours or overnight.

Once chilled, pour the ice cream base into an ice cream maker and churn according to the manufacturer's instructions. Transfer to a freezer-safe container and freeze until ready to combine with the sorbet.

To make the strawberry sorbet base, purée the strawberries in a blender or food processor until small chunks remain. Pour into a medium saucepan and add the remaining ingredients. Place over medium heat and warm until the sugar is dissolved (do not allow the strawberries to completely break down), about 8 minutes. Cover and completely chill in the refrigerator. Once cooled, pour into an ice cream maker and churn according to the manufacturer's instructions.

When both the sweet cream base and the sorbet base have been churned, gently layer into a freezer-safe container, which will produce a marbling effect when scooped. Do not stir or the ice cream will look muddy. Freeze until firm, at least 4 hours.

Banana Pudding Ice Cream
Inspired by Sam & Greg's, Huntsville, Alabama

MAKES 1½ QUARTS (1.4L)

There are plenty of banana-based desserts, but none are as dear to the hearts of Southerners as banana pudding. To this day, some Southern men claim to marry wives based on their ability to make banana pudding! The best banana puddings are made with real bananas, and the same is true for ice creams. Banana gives ice cream a gloriously creamy texture while imparting sweetness. Add a pinch of nutmeg, a touch of lemon and a generous amount of vanilla wafers and you are left with a frozen version of the South's favorite dessert.

2 egg yolks

1 ¾ cups (414ml) heavy cream

1 ¾ cups (414ml) whole milk

⅔ cup (133g) sugar

⅛ tsp salt

2 ripe bananas

Pinch of nutmeg

1 tsp lemon juice

½ tsp vanilla extract

1 ½ cups (240g) chopped vanilla wafers

Fill a large bowl with ice water. Whisk the egg yolks in a small bowl and set aside. Combine the cream, milk, sugar and salt in a medium saucepan and warm over medium heat until the mixture is hot and the sugar dissolves, 4 minutes. Temper the eggs by slowly pouring ½ cup (118ml) of the warmed cream mixture into the yolks, whisking constantly until combined. Return the warmed yolks to the pan with the remaining cream mixture. Heat the custard over medium-low heat, stirring constantly, until the custard thickens and coats the back of a spoon. Remove from the heat and pour through a fine-mesh sieve into a medium bowl.

Cut the bananas into chunks and purée in a blender with the nutmeg and lemon juice until smooth. Add the hot milk mixture and blend to combine. Pour the custard into a medium bowl. Place the bowl in the ice water bath and cool, about 20 minutes, whisking occasionally. Add the vanilla and stir to combine. Cover and refrigerate until well chilled, at least 4 hours or overnight. Freeze the vanilla wafers overnight.

Once chilled, pour the ice cream base into an ice cream maker and churn according to the manufacturer's instructions. When churning is complete, gently fold in the vanilla wafers. Transfer to a freezer-safe container and freeze until firm, at least 4 hours.

Peanut Butter Cookie Ice Cream
Inspired by Mike's Ice Cream, Nashville, Tennessee

MAKES 1 QUART (940ML)

Peanut butter is a versatile spread that is sweet, nutty, salty and satisfying. You can spread it on bread, fruit, chocolate or pretty much anything sweet. If I could only chose one food to take with me to a desert island, it would be peanut butter (delicious and practical). Exploding with peanut butter flavor with its creamy peanut butter base and chunks of peanut butter–filled peanut butter cookies, this scoop is one of my favorites.

1 ½ cups (355ml) whole milk, divided

1 tbsp (9g) cornstarch

½ cup (90g) unsalted natural peanut butter

½ teaspoon salt

1 ¾ cups (414ml) heavy cream

⅔ cup (133g) sugar

1 ¼ cups (150g) peanut butter–filled cookies

Fill a large bowl with ice water. In a small bowl, combine 2 tablespoons (30ml) of the milk with the cornstarch, whisk and set aside. Whisk the peanut butter and salt in a medium bowl and set aside.

Combine the remaining 1 cup and 6 tablespoons (325ml) milk with the heavy cream and sugar in a medium saucepan. Place over medium heat and bring the milk mixture to a low boil. Cook until the sugar dissolves, 3 minutes. Remove from the heat and gradually whisk in the cornstarch mixture. Return to a boil and cook over moderately high heat until the mixture is slightly thickened, about 1 minute. Pour into the bowl with the peanut butter and whisk until smooth. Set the bowl in the ice water bath to cool, 20 minutes, whisking occasionally. Cover and refrigerate until well chilled, at least 4 hours or overnight. Finely chop ¼ cup (30g) of the peanut butter–filled cookies and coarsely chop the remaining 1 cup (120g) cookies. Freeze the cookies overnight.

Once chilled, pour the ice cream base into an ice cream maker and churn according to the manufacturer's instructions. Halfway through churning, add the ¼ cup (30g) finely chopped peanut butter–filled cookies to the ice cream and continue churning. When churning is complete, gently fold in the remaining 1 cup (120g) peanut butter–filled cookies. Transfer to a freezer-safe container and freeze until firm, at least 4 hours.

Bourbon Ball Ice Cream
The Comfy Cow, Louisville, Kentucky

MAKES 1 QUART (940ML)

It is hard to think of Kentucky without thinking of bourbon. Bourbon ball candy is an old Kentucky tradition dating back to 1939. During the state capitol's sesquicentennial, a well-known dignitary stated that the two best tastes in all the world were chocolate and fine Kentucky bourbon. Mrs. Ruth Booe reportedly heard this comment and spent the next two years perfecting a chocolate and bourbon candy—the bourbon ball. The owners of Comfy Cow feel like this flavor is a tasty representation of Kentucky and its traditions.

ICE CREAM BASE

1 ¼ cups (295ml) whole milk, divided

2 ¼ cups (532ml) heavy cream, divided

1 large egg yolk

¾ cup (150g) granulated sugar

2 pinches of salt

1 tsp vanilla extract

2 tbsp (30ml) honey

3 tbsp (45ml) bourbon

1 cup (150g) chopped bourbon ball candies

BOURBON BALL CANDIES

¼ cup (57g) unsalted butter, softened

2 cups (260g) confectioners' sugar, divided

2 tbsp (30ml) bourbon

1 cup (180g) semisweet chocolate chips

To make the ice cream base, pour ½ cup (118ml) of the milk and 1 cup (237ml) of the cream into a medium bowl and set aside. Combine the remaining ¾ cup (177ml) milk and 1 ¼ cups (295ml) heavy cream with the egg yolk in a medium bowl and whisk to combine. Whisk the granulated sugar and salt into the cream and egg mixture. Pour into a medium saucepan and cook over medium heat. Cook, stirring constantly, until the mixture thickens slightly and lightly coats the back of a spoon (170°F [77°C]). Pour the custard through a fine-mesh strainer into the bowl with the reserved cream and milk. Stir in the vanilla, honey and bourbon. Cover and refrigerate until well chilled, at least 4 hours or overnight.

To make the bourbon ball candies, cream the butter in a stand mixer until completely smooth and no lumps are present. Mixing on medium-low speed, gradually add 1 ¾ cups (228g) of the confectioners' sugar, about ½ cup (65g) at a time, allowing the sugar to fully incorporate into the butter before each new addition. Stream in the bourbon and beat well. Transfer to an airtight container and chill for at least 1 hour.

Once chilled, scoop out 1 tablespoon (15g) of the bourbon ball mixture and drop into the remaining ¼ cup (32g) confectioners' sugar. Cover with a light coating of confectioners' sugar, then roll into a ball and place on a parchment-lined pan. Continue until all the balls are formed. Freeze for at least 2 hours.

Melt the chocolate chips using a double boiler. Gently dip the bottom of each ball into the chocolate and place on waxed paper. Freeze until the chocolate has hardened, then dip the candies fully to coat. Freeze again until the chocolate is hard. Refrigerate in a covered container. Once ready, chop the candies. Keep frozen until read to add ice cream.

Once the ice cream base is chilled, pour it into an ice cream maker and churn according to the manufacturer's instructions. When churning is complete, gently fold in the chopped bourbon ball candies. Transfer to a freezer-safe container and freeze until firm, at least 4 hours.

THE SCOOPABLE NORTHEAST

Connecticut, Maine, Massachusetts, New Hampshire, New Jersey, New York, Pennsylvania, Rhode Island, Vermont

The Northeast is where America was born. Settlers staked their independence in this region with pivotal events like Washington's Crossing of the Delaware, the Boston Tea Party in Massachusetts and the signing of the Declaration of Independence in Philadelphia.

Stretching from the farmland of Pennsylvania through the mountains of Maine, this region is also rich with ice cream history. The first ice cream parlors in America opened in New York. The first "home" hand-cranked ice cream maker was produced in Philadelphia. Now each state in the region boasts multiple ice cream shops, serving unique flavors such as Seaport Salty Swirl in Connecticut, Sweet Basil in New Jersey and Popcorn in New Hampshire.

You may have to take a plane ride or road trip to explore the colonial history of America, but turn the pages of this cookbook to take a ride through the variety of ice creams available in the Northeast.

Sweet Basil Ice Cream
The Bent Spoon, Princeton, New Jersey

MAKES ABOUT 1 QUART (940ML)

Sweet Basil Ice Cream has been a seasonal favorite at The Bent Spoon since 2005. The owners truly believe that New Jersey is the "Garden State," and nothing says summer more then the fragrant herb sweet basil. Adding fresh cream and a little sugar to the richness of local dark-yolk farm eggs brings out a flavor that is exceptionally complementary to many other seasonal flavors. This ice cream is likely to be a flavor you will look forward to every summer!

1 large egg

2 large egg yolks

1 ½ cups (355ml) whole milk

¾ cup (150g) sugar

½ tsp salt

1 ½ cups (355ml) heavy cream, chilled

10 large basil leaves, rinsed and patted dry

1 tbsp (15ml) lemon juice

Lightly whisk the egg and egg yolks in a medium bowl. Combine the milk, sugar and salt in a medium saucepan and warm over medium heat until the mixture is hot and the sugar dissolves, 4 to 5 minutes. Temper the eggs by slowly pouring about ½ cup (118ml) of the warmed milk mixture into the yolks, whisking constantly until combined. Return the warmed yolks to the pan with the remaining milk mixture. Heat the custard over medium-low heat, stirring constantly, until the custard thickens and coats the back of a spoon. Remove from the heat and pour through a fine-mesh sieve into a medium bowl. Whisk in the chilled cream. Cover and refrigerate until well chilled, at least 4 hours or overnight.

When ready to churn the ice cream, combine the basil leaves, lemon juice and 1 cup (237ml) of the cooled custard in a blender and blend until smooth. Add the remaining custard and pulse until combined. Pour into an ice cream maker immediately and churn according to the manufacturer's instructions. Serve soft immediately or transfer to a freezer-safe container and freeze until firm, at least 4 hours.

Tip: Keep in mind that different herbs respond to heat and oxidation differently. This recipe calls for a quick blend and an immediate freeze because the bright green color will turn quickly if it does not get frozen right away.

Serving note: This ice cream pairs especially well with chocolate (try folding in a chopped chocolate bar or cocoa nibs). Use it as an à la mode on a summer berry crisp or plum tart or even in a cold dessert soup to add an unexpected layering of flavors that truly speaks to the season.

Raspberry and Red Currant Ice Cream

Susanna's Ice Cream and Sorbet, Sweet Berry Farm, Middletown, Rhode Island

MAKES 1 QUART (940ML)

Inspired by her English roots, Susanna Williams creates thoughtful recipes using flavors she finds locally in Rhode Island as well as abroad. Ingredients such as gooseberries, geranium and elderflower are unique flavors in her ice cream that remind her of home. This tart and sweet ice cream was inspired by Susanna's fondness for sweet raspberries in America and red currants she would frequently find in Europe.

1 lb (454g) red raspberries

¾ lb (340g) red currants (if you cannot find them fresh, substitue 1 cup [230 g] prepackaged frozen purée)

1 ½ tbsp (22ml) water

3 egg yolks

1 ¼ cups (295ml) heavy cream, divided

1 cup (200g) sugar

⅛ tsp vanilla extract

⅛ tsp kirsch (optional)

Begin by making the raspberry purée. Press the raspberries through a fine-mesh sieve to remove the seeds. Reserve ½ cup (118ml) of raspberry purée and store the remainder for other uses. Discard the seeds.

Place the red currants in a small saucepan. Add the water to the pan, and cook until the red currants are soft and cooked through, 5 to 6 minutes. Transfer the fruit to a food mill or a fine strainer to remove the seeds. Reserve 1 cup (237ml) of red currant purée and store the remainder for other uses.

Lightly whisk the egg yolks in a medium bowl. Combine ¾ cup (177ml) of the heavy cream and the sugar in a medium saucepan and warm over medium heat until the mixture is hot and the sugar dissolves, 4 to 5 minutes. Temper the eggs by slowly pouring about ½ cup (118ml) of the warmed cream mixture into the yolks, whisking constantly until combined. Return the warmed yolks to the pan with the remaining cream mixture. Heat the custard over medium-low heat, stirring constantly, until the custard thickens and coats the back of a spoon, or to 175°F (79°C) on an instant-read thermometer.

Remove from the heat and pour through a fine-mesh sieve into a medium bowl. Add the remaining ½ cup (118ml) heavy cream, vanilla and kirsch. Stir well and cool to room temperature. Once cool, add the fruit purées. Mix the custard and fruit together very thoroughly and taste for sweetness. Add up to 2 tablespoons (25 g) sugar if additional sweetness is necessary. Chill the mixture for several hours or overnight.

When the ice cream base is chilled, pour into an ice cream maker and churn according to the manufacturer's instructions. Transfer to a freezer-safe container and freeze until firm, at least 4 hours.

Seaport Salty Swirl Ice Cream
Mystic Drawbridge Ice Cream, Mystic, Connecticut

MAKES 1 GENEROUS QUART (940ML)

Sea shanties, Mystic Seaport and local pub fare were the inspiration for this sweet and salty creation. Made in a town steeped in maritime and ice cream history, this ice cream has so many sweet and salty layers it could be considered a meal! Ice cream production began in this small shop by the town drawbridge in the 1800s and changed hands several times over the next two hundred years. The current owners are the fourth shop owners at this landmark location, and they continue to make delicious and creative flavors like the owners before them.

ICE CREAM BASE

2 cups (473ml) heavy cream

¾ cup (177ml) milk

¾ cup (150g) sugar

⅛ tsp salt

¼ cup (40g) chopped salted peanuts

½ cup (90g) roughly chopped chocolate-covered pretzels

CARAMEL SAUCE

1 cup (200g) sugar

¾ cup (172g) unsalted butter, at room temperature

½ cup (118ml) heavy cream

1 ½ tsp (9g) sea salt

PEANUT BUTTER SAUCE

1 cup (180g) creamy peanut butter

2 tbsp (30ml) whole milk

2 tbsp (30ml) heavy cream

4 tbsp (60ml) honey

To make the ice cream base, fill a large bowl with ice water. In a medium saucepan, combine the cream, milk, sugar and salt. Heat the milk mixture over medium heat, bringing to a temperature of 170°F (77°C) on an instant-read thermometer (do not boil). Remove from the heat and pour into a medium bowl. Set the bowl in the ice water bath to cool, 20 minutes, whisking occasionally. Cover and chill overnight.

To make the caramel sauce, cook the sugar in a heavy-bottomed saucepan over medium heat. Do not touch the sugar until all edges begin to melt. Cook until the sugar begins to brown, stirring frequently, allowing it to reach a deep amber color. Remove from the heat and add the butter, stirring until dissolved (the mixture will bubble). Add the heavy cream and sea salt. Return to low heat and stir until the ingredients are combined, 1 minute. Cool to room temperature before adding to the ice cream. Use leftovers in various desserts or eat with a spoon.

To make the peanut butter sauce, place all the ingredients in a saucepan and warm over medium heat. Stir occasionally until the ingredients are combined and smooth, 2 to 3 minutes. Cool to room temperature before adding to the ice cream.

Once the base is chilled, pour it into an ice cream maker and churn according to the manufacturer's instructions. When the ice cream is nearing the end of churning, add the peanuts and chocolate-covered pretzels and complete churning. Spoon a small layer of caramel and peanut butter sauces into a freezer-safe container and lightly spoon a layer of ice cream on top. Continue to alternate layers of sauces and ice cream until the container is full, gently swirling with a spoon (careful not to muddy the ice cream). Freeze until firm, at least 4 hours.

Brigadeiro Ice Cream
Mount Desert Island Ice Cream, Bar Harbor, Maine

MAKES 1 ½ QUARTS (1.4L)

Brigadeiro is a very popular candy in Brazil, tasting like a combination of chocolate and dulce de leche. Flavors at Mount Desert Island Ice Cream are frequently inspired by desserts and treats from other countries. Owner Linda Parker especially loves looking to Brazil for flavor ideas, as it is one of her favorite countries to visit. Brigadeiro is traditionally rolled into balls and served as individual candy pieces; however, this recipe cooks the flavor into a sweet, salty, cannot-help-but-go-back-for-more ice cream.

1 ¼ cups (295ml) whole milk, divided

1 ⅔ cups (394ml) heavy cream

1 cup (237ml) evaporated milk

½ cup (100g) sugar

1 ¼ cups (295ml) sweetened condensed milk

3 tbsp + 1 tsp (24g) unsweetened cocoa

2 tsp (10g) unsalted butter

¼ tsp salt

Fill a large bowl with ice water. Combine 1 cup (237ml) of the milk, cream, evaporated milk and sugar in a medium saucepan and warm over medium heat. Bring the milk mixture to a low boil. Cook until the sugar dissolves, 3 minutes. Remove from the heat and set aside.

Combine the condensed milk, cocoa, butter, salt and remaining ¼ cup (59ml) milk in a medium saucepan. Warm over medium-low heat and cook until the ingredients are combined, 2 to 3 minutes. Raise the heat to medium and continue cooking until thickened, stirring constantly, about 5 minutes. Remove from the heat and pour into the pan with the milk mixture. Return the pan to medium heat, warming and whisking until all ingredients are incorporated. Remove from the heat and pour into a medium bowl. If lumps of cocoa powder remain in the base, use an immersion blender to incorporate the ingredients. Set the bowl in the ice water bath to cool, 20 minutes, whisking occasionally. Cover and refrigerate overnight.

Once chilled, pour the ice cream base into an ice cream maker and churn according to the manufacturer's instructions. Transfer to a freezer-safe container and freeze until firm, at least 4 hours.

Note: Add 1 teaspoon of fine sea salt to this recipe to make Salty Brigadeiro.

Earl Grey Sriracha© Ice Cream
Little Baby's Ice Cream, Philadelphia, Pennsylvania

MAKES 1 QUART (940ML)

Earl Grey tea, with its citrus and floral notes, is a tea originating in Southeast Asia. There are many variations of the story behind the tea, but most stories acknowledge that the tea was made as a gift to the second Earl Grey from a Chinese mandarin. The owners of Little Baby's Ice Cream describe the flavor of this scoop as the milk from Fruit Loops cereal with a garlicky spicy kick at the end. The initial citrus bite and subsequent sweet rush gently give way to the Sriracha's subtle heat as the ice cream melts on your tongue. Serve as a spicy and surprising addition to any afternoon tea.

- -

4 egg yolks

½ cup (100g) cane sugar

2 cups (473ml) whole milk

1 cup (237ml) heavy cream

2 tbsp (6g) traditional Earl Grey tea leaves

1 ½ tsp Sriracha (more to taste)

Whisk the egg yolks and sugar in a medium bowl until pale in color. In a small saucepan, combine the milk and cream and place over medium heat. Warm until the mixture begins to bubble. Turn down the heat to low, add the tea leaves and steep for 3 minutes. Pour the tea-infused milk through a fine-mesh sieve into a medium bowl.

Temper the eggs by slowly pouring ½ cup (118ml) of the warmed milk mixture into the yolks, whisking constantly until combined. Return the warmed yolks to a medium saucepan with the remaining tea-infused milk mixture. Heat the custard over medium-low heat, stirring constantly, until the custard thickens and coats the back of a spoon. Remove from the heat and pour through a fine-mesh sieve into a medium bowl. Cool to room temperature. Cover and refrigerate until well chilled, at least 4 hours or overnight.

Once chilled, add the Sriracha. Taste and add more if desired. Pour the ice cream base into an ice cream maker and churn according to the manufacturer's instructions. Transfer to a freezer-safe container and freeze until firm, at least 4 hours.

Note: Little Baby's Ice Cream prefers to use local ingredients in their ice cream, thus they recommended milk and cream from Trickling Springs Creamery in Chambersburg, Pennsylvania, and Earl Grey Fancy OP tea from Premium Steap Tea Shop in Philly. If you live in the area, seek out these premium ingredients.

Tip: If you already have Earl Grey tea bags in your pantry, no need to go out and buy loose leaves. Simply cut open the bags, measure the tea leaves and add directly to the ice cream base.

lu·lu !

[loo-loo] *noun*

A remarkable, outstanding
and wonderful object or thing

e.g. small batch, artisan ice cream

Mimosa Ice Cream
lu.lu Ice Cream, Bristol, Vermont

MAKES 1 QUART (940ML)

Featured as a modern-day Creamsicle, this ice cream was created to celebrate Mother's Day. The owners of lu.lu love brunch and mimosas, so they felt there was no better way to represent the traditional Mother's Day brunch experience than with Mimosa Ice Cream. Tart and tangy with the subtle flavor of Champagne, this celebratory scoop is enjoyed by all.

3 oranges

¾ cup (150g) sugar

1 cup (237ml) 2% milk

1 ½ cups (355ml) heavy cream

Pinch of salt

5 egg yolks

½ cup (118ml) Champagne

Fill a large bowl with ice water and set aside. Zest the oranges directly into a food processor or blender. Add the sugar and blend until the orange zest is very fine and the sugar is fragrant.

In a medium saucepan, warm the milk, orange-scented sugar, heavy cream and salt, stirring occasionally. When the mixture just begins to bubble around the edges, remove from the heat. Cover and let the mixture steep for 1 hour. Strain out the orange zest using a fine-mesh strainer and discard the zest. Return the orange-infused mixture to the saucepan over medium heat and warm until hot to the touch.

Lightly whisk the egg yolks in a medium bowl. Temper the eggs by slowly pouring ½ cup (118ml) of the warmed cream mixture into the yolks, whisking constantly until combined. Return the warmed yolks to the pan with the remaining cream mixture. Heat the custard over medium-low heat, stirring constantly, until the custard thickens and coats the back of a spoon, 5 minutes. Remove from the heat and pour through a fine-mesh sieve into a medium bowl. Set the bowl in the ice water bath to cool, 20 minutes, whisking occasionally. Cover and refrigerate overnight.

Once the base is thoroughly chilled, add the Champagne, stirring well to combine. Churn according to the manufacturer's instructions. Transfer to a freezer-safe container and freeze for at least 4 hours.

Popcorn Ice Cream

Adapted from recipe by Sugar & Ice Creamery, Barrington, New Hampshire

MAKES 1 QUART (940ML)

The Sugar & Ice Creamery family handcrafts rich and seasonal ice cream flavors at their shop in New Hampshire. Popcorn is an original, tried-and-true American treat that they could not wait to reinvent as an ice cream flavor. Inspired by history, the family learned that Americans in the 1800s frequently consumed popcorn as a breakfast cereal with milk and sweetener. The shop developed an ice cream recipe by popping the best kernels to create an explosive flavor that is smooth, rich and pure. They hope you enjoy this sweet and salty treat.

- -

ICE CREAM BASE

6 cups (1420ml) whole milk

Three 3 oz (170g) bags plain microwave popcorn (oil free and salt free), popped

⅔ cup (133g) sugar, divided

1 ¼ tsp gelatin

2 ½ tbsp (18g) nonfat dry milk

¾ cup (177ml) heavy cream

SALTED CARAMEL (OPTIONAL MIX-IN)

½ cup (118ml) heavy cream

1 ⅓ cups (267g) sugar

¼ cup (59ml) water

6 tbsp (86g) salted butter

1 ½ tsp table salt

To make the ice cream base, pour the milk into a large saucepan and place over medium heat. Heat the milk to 165°F (74°C) on an instant-read thermometer. Remove the milk from the heat and add the freshly popped popcorn, stirring constantly to make sure all of the popcorn is submerged. This process may need to be repeated multiple times due to the quantity of popcorn. After all of the popcorn has been added to the milk, cover and steep for 15 minutes. Do not exceed 15 minutes because the popcorn will thicken the mixture, making it more difficult to extract the milk.

Fill a large bowl with ice water and set aside. When steeping is complete, pass the milk through a fine-mesh sieve into a medium bowl to remove all of the kernels. This process should yield about 2 ½ cups (592ml) of popcorn milk. If you are short, add a little more whole milk to equal 2 ½ cups (592ml). Place the bowl of popcorn milk over the ice water bath, whisking occasionally until cool, about 20 minutes. Cover and refrigerate for at least 4 hours, but no more than 12 hours.

Once again fill a large bowl with ice water and set aside. Mix 4 teaspoons (16g) of the sugar and gelatin in a small bowl and set aside. Pour the chilled popcorn milk into a medium saucepan and place over medium heat. When the milk is warm to the touch (75°F [24°C]), add the nonfat dry milk and whisk constantly until dissolved. Add the remaining sugar and whisk until dissolved, 1 to 2 minutes. Add the heavy cream and stir to combine. Add the gelatin-sugar mixture and stir in slow motion until the milk reaches 120°F (49°C). Increase the heat to medium-high and heat until it reaches 185°F (85°C). Remove from the heat and cook for 2 more minutes while whisking constantly. Pour through a fine-mesh sieve into a medium bowl and place over the ice water bath, whisking occasionally until cool, about 20 minutes. Cover and cool completely in the refrigerator, at least 4 hours.

(continued)

When the base is completely cool, whisk until smooth. Pour into an ice cream maker and churn according to the manufacturer's instructions. Transfer to a freezer-safe container and freeze for at least 4 hours. *For a caramel corn experience, lightly swirl in the salted caramel after churning (recipe below).*

To make the salted caramel, pour the heavy cream into a small saucepan. Bring to a simmer over medium heat. Thoroughly combine the sugar and water in a medium saucepan, achieving the consistency of wet sand. Bring to a boil over high heat. Cook until the sugar begins to brown, stirring frequently, allowing it to reach a deep amber color (338°F [170°C]). Turn off the heat and slowly stir in the hot heavy cream. Once the cream has been added, return the saucepan to high heat. Stir in the salted butter and table salt. Continue stirring until the caramel is smooth. Cool to room temperature before adding to the ice cream. Caramel can be reserved for later use and stored for up to 1 month in a cool, dry place. Do not keep in the refrigerator.

Sweet as Honey Ice Cream
Ample Hills Creamery, Brooklyn, New York

MAKES 1 GENEROUS QUART (940ML)

Made with local honey from Queens County Farm, this pleasingly sweet cream ice cream is laced with golden honeycomb. Inspired by everyone's favorite bear and his love of honey, the original ice cream included honeycomb and gummy bears, but trial and error revealed the gummy bears became too hard when frozen, and thus honey became the feature of this ice cream. Now it is perfect in its simplicity—creamy, crunchy and gooey all at the same time. The longer the morsels of honeycomb sit in the ice cream, the more the honeycomb will melt and flavor the ice cream. The resulting flavor is texturally complex and delightfully sweet. Be sure to wear oven mitts while whisking and pouring the molten honey!

ICE CREAM BASE

2 egg yolks

1 cup (200g) cane sugar

¾ cup (87g) nonfat dry milk

1 ¾ cups (414ml) whole milk

1 ¾ cups (414ml) heavy cream

HONEYCOMB CANDY

Makes 2 to 3 cups

1 cup (200g) cane sugar

⅓ cup (79ml) water

2 tbsp (30ml) honey

3 ½ tbsp (52ml) golden syrup

2 tsp baking soda

To make the ice cream base, fill a large bowl with ice water. Lightly whisk the egg yolks in a medium bowl and set aside. In a large saucepan, combine the sugar and nonfat milk, then add the whole milk. Blend these ingredients with a hand mixer or whisk until incorporated and the dry milk is dissolved. Add the cream. Heat the mixture gradually over medium heat, stirring frequently.

Temper the eggs by slowly pouring ½ cup (118ml) of the warmed cream mixture into the yolks, whisking constantly until combined. Return the warmed yolks to the pan with the remaining cream mixture. Heat the custard over medium-low heat, stirring constantly, until the custard thickens and coats the back of a spoon (165°F [74°C]) on an instant-read thermometer. Remove from the heat and pour through a fine-mesh sieve into a medium bowl. Set the bowl in the ice water bath to cool, 20 minutes, whisking occasionally. Cover and refrigerate until well chilled, at least 4 hours or overnight.

To make the honeycomb candy, butter a large baking sheet and then line it with parchment paper or use a silicone mat. In a large (8-quart [7.2L]) pot, heat the sugar, water, honey and syrup over high heat until it reaches 300°F (149°C) on a candy thermometer or high-temperature instant thermometer, stirring frequently until the mixture comes to a boil. Heating should take about 10 minutes. The mixture will drastically change color as it is heated and begin to look orange. Premeasure the baking soda and set aside.

(continued)

The moment the mixture hits 300°F (149°C), turn off the heat and whisk in the baking soda while wearing an oven mitt. Whisk the baking soda into the mixture vigorously and quickly to fully incorporate, then stop and watch the baking soda work its magic. Don't whisk too long—the longer you whisk, the less honeycomb will grow because you are beating out the air.

Initially, the mixture will quickly rise and then start to slow and pop. Once the mixture has finished rising, pour the honeycomb onto the prepared baking sheet and let rest until cooled, at least 30 minutes. The mixture will be extremely hot and orange and look like the surface of the moon. Once cool, break into pieces, transfer to a container and freeze until ready to use (the honey will begin to dissolve unless it is kept in the freezer). Chop into small pieces before incorporating 1 cup (160 g) into the ice cream. Freeze any leftover candy for use in future ice creams.

Churn the ice cream base according to the manufacturer's instructions. When churning is complete, gently fold in the honeycomb pieces. Transfer to a freezer-safe container and freeze until firm, at least 4 hours.

Pennsylvania Dutch Chocolate–Covered Pretzel Ice Cream

Inspired by Gerenser's Exotic Ice Cream, New Hope, Pennsylvania

MAKES 1 QUART (940ML)

In addition to the cheesesteak, Philadelphia is a city famous for its soft pretzels. Philadelphians are rumored to consume twelve times as many pretzels as the average U.S. citizen, and the city boasts a pretzel museum. Given that cheesesteak ice cream would taste pretty bad, chocolate pretzel ice cream was the go-to flavor for Bob Gerenser to best represent "The City of Brotherly Love." Situated in a small town outside of Philly, Gerenser's has been serving classic and exotic ice cream flavors for 55 years. He knows how to make a winning dessert.

CHOCOLATE LIQUOR

⅓ cup (37g) cocoa powder

⅓ cup (79ml) water

⅓ cup (67g) sugar

2 oz (56g) bittersweet chocolate, chopped

ICE CREAM BASE

1 ¾ cups (414ml) whole milk, divided

1 tbsp (9g) cornstarch

1 ½ cups (355ml) heavy cream, divided

⅓ cup (67g) sugar

½ tsp sea salt

½ tsp vanilla extract

1 cup (180g) chopped chocolate-covered pretzels

To make the chocolate liquor, combine the cocoa powder, water and sugar in a small saucepan over medium heat and bring to a low boil, whisking constantly. As soon as you see bubbles, remove from the heat and add the chopped chocolate. Let sit for 2 minutes, and then stir the chocolate liquor until smooth. Pour into a medium bowl and set aside.

To make the ice cream base, fill a large bowl with ice water and set aside. In a small bowl, combine 2 tablespoons (30ml) of the milk with the cornstarch, whisk and set aside. Combine the remaining milk, ½ cup (118ml) of the cream, sugar and salt in a medium saucepan and place over medium heat. Bring the milk mixture to a low boil. Cook until the sugar dissolves, 3 minutes.

Remove the milk mixture from the heat and gradually whisk in the cornstarch mixture. Return to a boil and cook over moderately high heat until the mixture is slightly thickened, about 1 minute. Pour the base into the chocolate liquor and whisk to combine. Stir in remaining 1 cup (237ml) cream. Set the bowl in the ice water bath to cool, 20 minutes, whisking occasionally. Once cool, add the vanilla. Refrigerate the ice cream base until chilled, at least 4 hours or overnight.

Pour the base into an ice cream machine and churn according to the manufacturer's instructions. When churning is complete, gently fold in the chocolate-covered pretzel pieces. Transfer to a freezer-safe container and freeze until firm, at least 4 hours.

Coffee Ice Cream Sandwich Ice Cream

Toscanini's Ice Cream, Cambridge, Massachusetts

MAKES 1 GENEROUS QUART (940ML)

Coffee ice cream is an extremely popular ice cream flavor in Massachusetts. Every ice cream shop in the region serves the classic flavor, but owner Gus Toscanini wanted to add a special twist. He looked to his Italian roots for inspiration. Italians often serve redundant dishes, such as starchy pizza with starchy pasta, so Gus thought it would be fun to serve ice cream with ice cream. Ice cream sandwiches offer a soft bite of childhood in every scoop of this ice cream. Enjoy this spin on a classic flavor and let it take you back to the good ol' days.

3 standard ice cream sandwiches

1 ½ cups (355ml) half-and-half, divided

5 egg yolks

1 ½ cups (355ml) whole milk

¾ cup (150g) sugar

1 tsp vanilla extract

¼ cup (14g) instant coffee

Unwrap the ice cream sandwiches, and using a large knife, chop the sandwiches into small pieces. Put the pieces back into the freezer and reserve.

Pour 1 cup (237ml) of the half-and-half into a medium bowl and set aside. Lightly whisk the egg yolks in a small bowl. Combine the whole milk, remaining ½ cup (118ml) half-and-half and sugar in a small saucepan and place over medium-low heat. Stay attentive and stir gently. Stop heating when a white edge appears around the liquid, lining the inside of the pan, 4 to 5 minutes. Temper the eggs by slowly pouring the warmed milk mixture into the yolks, whisking constantly until combined. Return the custard to the pan and heat over medium-low heat, stirring constantly, until the custard thickens and coats the back of a spoon. Remove from the heat and pour through a fine-mesh sieve into the bowl containing the half-and-half. Stir to combine. Cool to room temperature. Cover and refrigerate until well chilled, at least 4 hours or overnight.

Once completely cool, add the vanilla and instant coffee; stir to combine. Pour the ice cream base into an ice cream maker and churn according to the manufacturer's instructions. When churning is complete, fold in the ice cream sandwich pieces. Pack the ice cream into a freezer-safe container. Freeze until firm, at least 4 hours.

THE MOUTHWATERING MIDWEST

Illinois, Indiana, Iowa, Kansas, Michigan, Minnesota, Missouri, Nebraska, North Dakota, Ohio, South Dakota, Wisconsin

Encompassing a large swath of land that captures the wide-open plains through the states of the Great Lakes, the Midwest is a region full of good people and good food. American home cooking and comfort food seem to be the specialties of this region. Although the cooking in the Midwest may revolve around the classics, the ice cream from this region is anything but typical. With inventive flavors such as Thai Peanut Curry from Kansas, Dark Chocolate Zin from Minnesota, Olive Oil Gelato with Sea Salt from North Dakota, and Chai Pink Peppercorn from Wisconsin, the recipes in the chapter are sure to please the palate as much as Mom's meat and potatoes.

America's heartland provides much of the dairy, grains and meat to the remainder of the country. These ingredients are mixed into food classics and comforts ranging from pizza to chili to barbecue. Take a look at this chapter and find a range of ice cream to suit any comfort your heart desires.

Dark Chocolate Zin Ice Cream
Adapted from recipe by Izzy's Ice Cream, Minneapolis, Minnesota

MAKES ABOUT 1 QUART (940ML)

As a lover of chocolate truffles, owner Jeff Sommers frequently finds himself eating chocolate. While sampling different flavors from a local chocolatier's supply, he left his tasting determined to create an ice cream that would be as equally delicious. After many hours in the kitchen, Dark Chocolate Zin Ice Cream was born. Beginning with a decadent chocolate base and adding a fruity hint of wine and the light tanginess of balsamic vinegar, this flavor is sure to satisfy any chocolate or wine lover.

CHOCOLATE LIQUOR
¾ cup (83g) cocoa powder

⅓ cup (79ml) water

⅓ cup (79ml) red zinfandel

¼ cup (50g) sugar

1 oz (28g) dark chocolate, chopped

ICE CREAM BASE
3 egg yolks

2 ¼ cups (532ml) heavy cream, divided

1 cup (237ml) whole milk

½ cup (100g) sugar

Pinch of salt

1 tsp (5ml) vanilla extract

3 tsp (15ml) balsamic vinegar, divided

¼ cup (59ml) red zinfandel

To make the chocolate liquor, combine the cocoa powder, water, wine and sugar in a small saucepan. Place the saucepan over low heat and bring to a low boil, whisking constantly. As soon as you see bubbles, remove from the heat and add the dark chocolate. Let sit for 2 minutes, and then stir the chocolate liquor until smooth. Pour into a medium bowl and set aside.

To make the ice cream base, fill a large bowl with ice water and set aside. Lightly whisk the egg yolks in a medium bowl and set aside. Combine 1 cup (237ml) of the cream, milk, sugar and salt in a medium saucepan and place over medium-low heat. Warm to dissolve the sugar, about 5 minutes (do not boil). Temper the eggs by slowly pouring the warmed cream mixture into the yolks, whisking constantly until combined. Return the custard to the pan and stir in the remaining 1 ¼ cups (295ml) cream. Warm over medium-low heat, stirring constantly, until the custard thickens and coats the back of a spoon, 8 minutes.

Remove the custard from the heat and pour through a fine-mesh sieve into the chocolate liquor. Add the vanilla and whisk to combine. Set the bowl in the ice water bath to cool, 20 minutes, whisking occasionally. Once cool, add 1 teaspoon (5ml) of the vinegar and stir to incorporate. Cover and refrigerate until well chilled, at least 4 hours or overnight.

Once chilled, pour the ice cream base into an ice cream maker and churn according to the manufacturer's instructions. When the ice cream has begun to freeze but is not completely frozen, slowly pour in the remaining 2 teaspoons (10ml) vinegar and wine. Complete churning. Transfer the ice cream to a freezer-safe container and freeze overnight.

Note: Quality ice cream is made from quality ingredients. Izzy's owners prefer to use high-end ingredients, such as Guittard chocolate and cocoa powder, Ravenswood red zinfandel, Modena Number 2 balsamic vinegar, and Bourbon-Indonesian vanilla extract.

Chai Pink Peppercorn Ice Cream
Adapted from recipe by Purple Door Ice Cream, Milwaukee, Wisconsin

MAKES 1 QUART (940ML)

The folks at Purple Door were inspired to make this ice cream while wandering the aisles of the Spice House in Milwaukee. Filled to the brim with spices from around the world, the Spice House is bursting with inspiration. A conversation between shop owners resulted in the creation of a warm spice blend that mingles perfectly with sweet cream. Pink peppercorns are added to give a slightly floral flavor to the mix. Try the homemade version of this sweet and spicy ice cream and become inspired.

CHAI SPICE MIX

1 tsp ground cinnamon

1 tsp ground ginger

1 tsp ground cardamom

½ tsp ground cloves

½ tsp ground star anise

¼ tsp ground black pepper

ICE CREAM BASE

2 cups (473ml) whole milk, divided

2 tsp tapioca starch

1 tsp whole pink peppercorns

1 ¼ cups (295ml) heavy cream

⅔ cup (133g) sugar

1 ¼ tsp chai spice mix

¾ tsp vanilla extract

To prepare the chai spice mix, place all the ingredients in a small bowl and whisk to combine. Set aside.

To make the ice cream base, in a small bowl, mix 2 tablespoons (30ml) of the milk with the tapioca starch and set aside. Crush the pink peppercorns using a mortar and pestle or heavy rolling pin; set aside. Combine the remaining milk, cream, sugar and chai spice mix in a medium saucepan and place over medium heat. Bring the milk mixture to a low boil. Cook until the sugar dissolves, 3 minutes.

Remove the milk mixture from the heat and gradually whisk in the tapioca starch mixture. Return to a boil and cook over moderately high heat until the mixture is slightly thickened, about 1 minute. Pour into a medium bowl and add the pink peppercorns. Cool to room temperature. Add the vanilla. Cover and refrigerate until well chilled, at least 4 hours or overnight.

Once chilled, whisk and pour the ice cream base into an ice cream maker and churn according to the manufacturer's instructions. Transfer to a freezer-safe container and freeze until firm, at least 4 hours.

Note: Feel free to use your favorite chai spice mix in place of the recipe above. Use leftover spice mix in tea, hot beverages, on top of cereal, in oatmeal or in any other dish that could use a little sweet spice!

Shayla Mae's Peanut Butter Truffle Ice Cream

Adapted from recipe by Kimmer's Ice Cream, St. Charles, Illinois

MAKES 1 QUART (940ML)

When Kimberly Elam opened up her ice cream shop straight out of college, she needed a right-hand guy (or girl). She met up with her longtime friend Shayla and the rest was history. Shayla Mae's Peanut Butter Truffle flavor was a creation in their first year of business and the flavor still remains a customer favorite. As peanut butter enthusiasts themselves, Kimberly and Shayla are not surprised by the success of this flavor. With decadent peanut butter ice cream laced with swirls of thick chocolate truffle, how could you go wrong?

ICE CREAM BASE

1 cup (237ml) whole milk, divided

1 tbsp + 1 tsp (13g) tapioca starch

2 cups (473ml) heavy cream, divided

¾ cup (150g) sugar

2 tbsp (30ml) honey

⅔ cup (120g) creamy peanut butter

2 tsp (10ml) vanilla extract

TRUFFLE SWIRL

½ cup (118ml) heavy cream

6 oz (170g) semisweet chocolate chips

To make the ice cream base, in a small bowl, whisk ¼ cup (59ml) of the milk and the tapioca starch and set aside. Combine the remaining ¾ cup (178ml) milk, 1 cup (237ml) of the cream, sugar and honey in a medium saucepan and warm over medium-high heat. Bring the milk mixture to a low boil. Cook until the sugar dissolves, 3 minutes.

Remove the milk mixture from the heat and gradually whisk in the tapioca starch mixture. Return to a boil and cook over moderately high heat until the mixture is slightly thickened, about 2 minutes. Remove from the heat and add the peanut butter. Whisk to combine. Pour into a medium bowl and add the remaining 1 cup (237ml) cream and vanilla. Stir, cover and refrigerate until well chilled, at least 4 hours or overnight.

To make the truffle swirl, heat the heavy cream in a microwave for 30 seconds to 1 minute (until hot). Remove the cream from the microwave and add the chocolate chips. Allow the mixture to sit for a couple minutes so the chocolate chips melt. Stir to combine. Refrigerate until firm.

Once the ice cream base is chilled, pour into an ice cream maker and churn according to the manufacturer's instructions. Remove the truffle swirl from refrigerator while the ice cream is churning. Do not over churn—the ice cream may begin to look grainy, at which point stop churning. Spoon a small layer of truffle swirl into a freezer-safe container and lightly spoon a layer of ice cream on top. Continue to alternate layers of swirl and ice cream until the container is full, swirling with a spoon. Freeze until firm, at least 4 hours.

Nebraska Sweet Corn Ice Cream
Ted & Wally's, Omaha, Nebraska

MAKES 1 QUART (940ML)

Growing up in a diverse family gave the owners of this Omaha-based ice cream shop an opportunity to enjoy a variety of foods as children. Several ice cream flavors in their shop are inspired by their childhood foods, creating an intimate connection to their recipes. As children of a corn-growing father, they grew up shucking, cleaning and eating the sweet vegetable. They, like many other Nebraskans, take pride in their corn, which is so sweet it works perfectly as the "sugar" for their ice cream. They hope you enjoy this taste of their home.

2 egg yolks

1 cup (237ml) whole milk

¾ cup (150g) sugar

2 cups (473ml) heavy cream

1 ½ tbsp (22g) salted butter, melted

Generous pinch of salt

Pinch of ground black peppercorns

1 cup (163g) fresh sweet corn kernels, plus optional ⅓ cup (54g) for mixing

Lightly whisk the egg yolks in a medium bowl and set aside. Combine the milk and sugar in a medium saucepan and warm over medium heat until the mixture is hot and the sugar dissolves, 4 to 5 minutes. Temper the eggs by slowly pouring ½ cup (118ml) of the warmed milk mixture into the yolks, whisking constantly until combined. Return the warmed yolks to the pan with the remaining milk mixture. Heat the custard over medium-low heat, stirring constantly, until the custard thickens and coats the back of a spoon.

Remove the custard from the heat and pour through a fine-mesh sieve into a medium bowl. Add the heavy cream, melted butter, salt and pepper (adjust to taste). Pour this entire mixture into a blender with 1 cup (163g) of the corn kernels and purée until smooth. Cover and refrigerate until well chilled, at least 4 hours or overnight.

Once chilled, pour the base into your ice cream maker and churn according to the manufacturer's instructions. If you like some crunch in your ice cream, add the optional ⅓ cup (54g) fresh corn kernels just before the ice cream is finished churning, and then complete the churning process. Transfer to a freezer-safe container and freeze for 4 hours or overnight.

Serving note: Pairs well with tart berries, such as a blackberry or raspberry compote.

Thai Peanut Curry Ice Cream
Glacé Artisan Ice Cream, Leawood, Kansas

MAKES 1½ QUARTS (1.4L)

Owner Christopher Elbow frequently enjoys cooking Thai and other Asian food in his home, and curries are one of his family's favorites. After eating a delicious curry one evening, he enjoyed a scoop of vanilla ice cream for dessert and quickly noticed that the cooling effect of the ice cream blended well with the lingering spice from his dinner. The next day, Chris brought curry paste into his shop and started working on incorporating the complex flavors of Thai curry into an ice cream. The recipe worked fabulously and the flavor is one of his all-time favorites the shop has produced to date.

2 cups (473ml) whole milk

1 cup (237ml) heavy cream

1 cup (237ml) unsweetened coconut milk

1 ¼ cups (250g) sugar, divided

2 tbsp (30ml) Thai Massaman Yellow Curry Paste*

10 large egg yolks

1 tbsp (15ml) vanilla extract

½ cup (80g) chopped toasted peanuts

Fill a large bowl with ice water. In a large saucepan, combine the milk, cream, coconut milk, ⅔ cup (133g) of the sugar and the curry paste. Place over medium heat. When small bubbles begin to form around the edges, remove from the heat and cover to let the curry flavor infuse, about 5 minutes.

Whisk the egg yolks and the remaining ⅓ cup + ¼ cup (117g) sugar in a medium bowl until pale in color. Temper the eggs by slowly pouring the curry-infused milk mixture into the yolks, whisking constantly until combined. Return the custard to the pan and heat over medium-low heat, stirring constantly, until the custard thickens and coats the back of a spoon, 3 to 4 minutes. Remove from the heat and pour through a fine-mesh sieve into a medium bowl. Set the bowl in the ice water bath to cool, 20 minutes, whisking occasionally. Whisk in the vanilla. Cover and refrigerate until well chilled, at least 4 hours or overnight.

Once chilled, pour the ice cream base into an ice cream maker and churn according to the manufacturer's instructions. When churning is complete, gently fold in the toasted peanuts. Transfer to a freezer-safe container and freeze until firm, at least 4 hours.

Christopher prefers Massaman Yellow Curry Paste because it features warm spices such as cinnamon and nutmeg along with the brightness of lemongrass and other classic ingredients. Other curry pastes will work in this recipe, but just be mindful about the level of spiciness. Feel free to adjust the amount of curry to suit your taste.

Key Lime Pie Ice Cream
Adapted from recipe by The Outside Scoop, Indianola, Iowa

MAKES 1 GENEROUS QUART (940ML)

Filled with the tart flavor of lime, decadent sweet cream and crunchy graham cracker, this scoop will remind you of a sunny summer day. Although Key lime pie is a dessert generally associated with Key West, Florida, greater availability of Key limes has made it possible to spread the love to other regions, including the Midwest. Inspired by delicious Key lime pie baked by the owner's mother, this flavor is a bright ray of sunshine on a cool winter day in Iowa. Try a scoop and you will be sure to smile.

KEY LIME SYRUP

6 tbsp (90ml) Key lime juice

¼ cup (50g) sugar

ICE CREAM BASE

2 egg yolks

1 ½ cups (355ml) skim milk

¼ cup (50g) sugar

½ cup (118ml) sweetened condensed milk

1 cup (237ml) heavy cream, chilled

GRAHAM CRACKER CRUST

1 ⅓ cups (120g) finely crushed graham crackers

¼ cup (50g) sugar

¼ cup (57g) unsalted butter, melted

To prepare the Key lime syrup, combine the juice and sugar in a small saucepan and place over medium heat. Heat until the sugar is dissolved, 1 to 2 minutes. Pour into a small bowl, cover and refrigerate until completely cool.

To prepare ice cream base, whisk the egg yolks in a medium bowl and set aside. Combine the skim milk, sugar and sweetened condensed milk in a medium saucepan and warm over medium heat until the mixture is hot and the sugar dissolves, 4 to 5 minutes. Temper the eggs by slowly pouring ½ cup (118ml) of the warmed milk mixture into the yolks, whisking constantly until combined. Return the warmed yolks to the pan with the remaining milk mixture. Heat the custard over medium-low heat, stirring constantly, until the custard thickens and coats the back of a spoon, 3 to 4 minutes. Remove from the heat and pour through a fine-mesh sieve into a medium bowl. Whisk in the chilled cream. Cover and refrigerate until well chilled, at least 4 hours or overnight.

To make the graham cracker crust, preheat the oven to 325°F (170°C, or gas mark 3). Mix the ingredients in a bowl. Press firmly into the bottom of an 8" (20.3cm) square baking pan. Bake for 10 minutes, or until the crust is slightly browned. Let the crust cool, then cut or crumble into small chunks. Chill completely before folding into the ice cream.

When ready to churn the ice cream, combine the ice cream base and Key lime syrup and whisk. Taste the base and if you would prefer more tartness, add more Key lime juice, 1 tablespoon (15ml) at a time. When the taste is to your liking, pour into an ice cream maker and churn according to the manufacturer's instructions. When churning is complete, gently fold in the graham cracker pieces or crust. Transfer to a freezer-safe container and freeze until firm, at least 4 hours.

Tip: No time to prepare graham cracker crust? Subtitute 1 cup (90 g) chopped graham crackers for an equally delicious treat.

Cow Patty Ice Cream
Young's Jersey Dairy, Yellow Springs, Ohio

MAKES ABOUT 1 QUART (940ML)

When you sit and enjoy a scoop at Young's Jersey Dairy, you do not have to look far to find the cows that provide the milk for the ice cream. And if you get too close you may be unfortunate enough to spy one of their cow patties! The owners laugh a little every day when customers ask about the flavor or order a scoop. You don't know about cow patties? Well let's just say this rich and chunky chocolate ice cream is a whole lot better than the real thing.

. . . .

2 egg yolks

2 cups (474ml) heavy cream

½ cup (118ml) Hershey's dark chocolate syrup

2 cups (474ml) milk

½ cup (100g) sugar

1 tbsp (6g) flour

¼ tsp salt

1 tbsp (7g) unsweetened cocoa powder

⅓ cup (60g) semisweet or bittersweet chocolate chips

⅓ cup (60g) crushed Butterfinger candy

3 Oreo cookies, crushed

Lightly whisk the egg yolks in a medium bowl and set aside. Whisk the cream and chocolate syrup in a medium bowl and set aside. Combine the milk, sugar, flour, salt and cocoa in a medium saucepan and place over medium heat. Warm until the mixture is hot and the sugar dissolves, 4 to 5 minutes. Temper the eggs by slowly pouring ½ cup (118ml) of the warmed milk mixture into the yolks, whisking constantly until combined. Return the warmed yolks to the pan with the remaining milk mixture. Heat the custard over medium-low heat, stirring constantly, until the custard thickens and coats the back of a spoon, 1 to 2 minutes.

Remove the custard from the heat and pour through a fine-mesh sieve into the bowl containing the cream and chocolate mixture. Stir to combine. Cool to room temperature. Cover and refrigerate until well chilled, at least 4 hours or overnight.

Once chilled, pour the ice cream base into an ice cream maker and churn according to the manufacturer's instructions. When churning is complete, gently fold in the chocolate chips, Butterfinger candy and Oreo cookies. Transfer to a freezer-safe container and freeze until firm, at least 4 hours.

Purple Cow Ice Cream
Adapted from recipe by Little Brick Ice Cream, Platte, South Dakota

MAKES 1 QUART (940ML)

Little Brick Ice Cream takes pride in trying to make someone's day a little better. Purple Cow Ice Cream was made for the older generation with memories of visiting the local drugstore and ordering a purple cow shake (vanilla ice cream plus grape juice). The flavor is also made for young children, who love to order by color. Purple Cow is all about having fun! Mix up this quick and easy ice cream for a sweet trip down memory lane.

1 cup (237ml) grape juice concentrate

1 ½ cups (355ml) whole milk

1 ½ cups (355ml) heavy cream

¼ cup (50g) sugar

Pour the grape juice concentrate into a medium bowl and set aside.

Combine the milk, cream and sugar in a medium saucepan and place over medium heat. Bring the milk mixture to a low boil. Cook until the sugar dissolves, 3 minutes. Remove from the heat and pour the cream mixture through a sieve into the grape juice concentrate. Cool to room temperature. Cover and refrigerate until well chilled, at least 4 hours or overnight.

Once chilled, pour the ice cream base into an ice cream maker and churn according to the manufacturer's instructions. Transfer to a freezer-safe container and freeze until firm, at least 4 hours.

Apple Butter Rummy Pecan Ice Cream

Hartzell's Ice Cream, Bloomington, Indiana

MAKES 1 ½ QUARTS (1.4L)

The story of this flavor began when owner Hartzell Martel traveled to the quaint artist town of Nashville, Indiana. There he tasted this first homemade apple butter and immediately thought it would be a great ingredient for ice cream. While he was developing the flavor for his shop, a good friend shared some Appleton Jamaican rum with Hartzell and he quickly decided that the spicy notes would pair well with the apple butter. The addition of allspice, cloves and pecans gives this scoop a comforting and warm feeling, especially welcome during the crisp fall and winter months in Indiana. Enjoy when you need a little bit of warmth or during any season.

ICE CREAM BASE

2 cups (473ml) whole milk, divided

1 ½ tsp (4g) cornstarch

1 ¼ cups (295ml) heavy cream

⅔ cup (134g) brown sugar

2 tbsp (30ml) light corn syrup

1 vanilla bean, split and scraped

1 ¼ cups (295ml) unsweetened apple butter

1 tsp (3g) freshly ground cinnamon

¼ tsp allspice*

⅛ tsp ground cloves*

⅛ tsp fine sea salt

2 to 3 tbsp (30 to 45ml) Appleton Jamaican rum

1 cup (120g) salted pecans (see below)

SALTED PECANS

1 tbsp (14g) unsalted butter

1 cup (120g) chopped pecans

¼ tsp sea salt

To make the ice cream base, fill a large bowl with ice water. In a small bowl, combine 2 tablespoons (30ml) of the milk with the cornstarch, whisk and set aside. In another large bowl, add the cream and set aside.

Combine the remaining milk with the brown sugar, corn syrup, vanilla bean scrapings and pod, apple butter, cinnamon, allspice, cloves and sea salt in a medium saucepan and place over medium heat. Bring the milk mixture to a low boil. Cook until the sugar dissolves, 3 minutes. Remove the milk mixture from the heat and gradually whisk in the cornstarch mixture. Return to a boil and cook over moderately high heat until the mixture is slightly thickened, about 1 minute. Remove from the heat and pour into the large bowl with the cream. Carefully remove the vanilla bean pod. Set the bowl in the ice water bath to cool, 20 minutes, whisking occasionally. Cover and refrigerate until well chilled, at least 4 hours or overnight.

To make the salted pecans, melt the butter in a heavy skillet over medium heat. Add the pecans and stir to coat. Sauté until the pecans begin to brown, about 5 minutes, stirring occasionally. Stir in the salt and remove from the heat. Cool completely before adding to the ice cream.

Once the ice cream base is chilled, add the rum, adjusting to taste. Pour into an ice cream maker and churn according to the manufacturer's instructions. When churning is complete, gently fold in the salted pecans. Transfer to a freezer-safe container and freeze until firm, at least 4 hours.

If you are using spiced apple butter, omit the cloves and allspice from the recipe.

Tip: Prefer the flavor of peaches? Substitute peach butter and bourbon for a sweet Southern-inspired treat.

Michigan Salad Ice Cream
Treat Dreams, Ferndale, Michigan

MAKES 1 GENEROUS QUART (940ML)

The folks at Treat Dreams are always trying to think outside the box when developing their flavors. A salad-type ice cream recently came to mind, and it was a natural to make an ice cream inspired by salads popular in the state. Most salads in Michigan include lettuce (which is thankfully omitted), tart cherries (Traverse City is one of the largest producers of tart cherries in the world), blue cheese or feta, and either walnuts or pecans. The ice cream version is sweet and salty and the perfect savory dinner accompaniment. A must-try for blue cheese lovers!

ICE CREAM BASE
4 large egg yolks

¾ cup (150g) sugar

2 ½ cups (592ml) heavy cream

1 ¼ cups (295ml) whole milk

8 oz (224g) crumbled blue cheese

¼ tsp salt

½ cup (80 g) dried cherries, halved

CANDIED PECANS
⅓ cup (67g) sugar

½ tsp ground cinnamon

½ tsp salt

1 egg white

1 ½ tsp (7.5ml) vanilla extract

8 oz (224g) pecan halves

To make the ice cream base, whisk the egg yolks and sugar in a bowl until thickened; set aside. In a medium saucepan, bring the cream and milk to a simmer over medium-low heat. Simmer for 10 minutes, then remove from the heat. Temper the eggs by slowly pouring 1 cup (237ml) of the warmed cream mixture into the yolks, whisking constantly until combined. Return the warmed yolks to the pan with the remaining cream mixture. Heat the custard over medium-low heat, stirring constantly, until the custard thickens and coats the back of a spoon (160°F [71°C]) on an instant-read thermometer. Add the crumbled blue cheese, whisking until melted, and remove from the heat. Pour through a fine-mesh sieve into a large bowl. Whisk in the salt. Cool to room temperature. Cover and refrigerate until well chilled, at least 4 hours or overnight.

To make the candied pecans, preheat the oven to 250°F (120°C, or gas mark ½). Spray a large baking sheet with cooking spray or line with a silicone mat. Set aside. Mix the sugar, cinnamon and salt in a bowl. Whisk the egg white and vanilla together in a separate bowl. Toss the pecans in the egg white mixture until coated. Add the sugar mixture to the pecan mixture, and stir until the pecans are coated. Spread the pecans on the prepared baking sheet. Bake, stirring every 15 minutes, until the pecans are browned, about 1 hour. Chop and cool completely before adding to ice cream.

When the ice cream base is chilled, pour into an ice cream maker and churn according to the manufacturer's instructions. When churning is complete, gently fold in ½ cup (64 g) of the candied pecans (save the remaining for another use) and the dried cherries. Transfer to a freezer-safe container and freeze until firm, at least 4 hours.

Olive Oil Gelato with Sea Salt
Fireflour Pizza, Bismarck, North Dakota

MAKES 1 QUART (940ML)

Fruity, grassy, buttery and peppery are all words to describe the unique flavor of olive oil. Each type of olive oil complements a different kind of dish. The fruity and light flavor of olive oil pairs very well with the sweet cream of ice cream, giving the scoop added creaminess and a smooth texture. When topped with a sprinkling of salt, the sweet and salty notes come alive. For some added crunch, serve with roasted pine nuts or sunflower seeds.

4 large egg yolks

⅔ cup (133g) sugar

2 cups (473ml) whole milk

1 cup (237ml) heavy cream

Pinch of salt, plus more for sprinkling

⅓ cup (79ml) extra virgin olive oil, plus more for drizzling

Fill a large bowl with ice water and set aside. Whisk the egg yolks and sugar in a medium bowl until pale in color; set aside. Combine the milk and cream in a medium saucepan and warm over medium heat until the mixture is hot and beginning to bubble, 3 to 4 minutes. Temper the eggs by slowly pouring ½ cup (118ml) of the warmed cream mixture into the yolks, whisking constantly until combined. Return the warmed yolks to the pan with the remaining cream mixture. Heat the custard over medium-low heat, stirring constantly, until the custard thickens and coats the back of a spoon. Remove from the heat and pour through a fine-mesh sieve into a medium bowl. Whisk in the salt. Set the bowl in the ice water bath to cool, 20 minutes, whisking occasionally. Cover and refrigerate until well chilled, at least 4 hours or overnight.

Once the ice cream base is chilled, add the olive oil and whisk until combined. Pour into an ice cream maker and churn according to the manufacturer's instructions. Transfer to a freezer-safe container and freeze until firm, at least 4 hours. Serve with a drizzle of olive oil on top of the scoop along with a sprinkle of sea salt.

Note: Find a good-quality fruity extra virgin olive oil for the recipe. It will make a big difference in the flavor!

Cookie Monster Ice Cream
Inspired by Serendipity Homemade Ice Cream, St. Louis, Missouri

MAKES 1 QUART (940ML)

Walk into any ice cream shop with children and they are often drawn to the most colorful flavors, with blue flavors at the top of the list. When owner Beckie Jacobs decided to make a blue flavor, she started with a cotton candy ice cream. One day she decided to mix in cookies so the flavor was reminiscent of the favorite Sesame Street character Cookie Monster, and now it is her most popular flavor. Bright blue and full of flavor, this ice cream is sure to please any color-loving child (or adult).

1 ½ cups (355ml) whole milk, divided

1 tbsp (9g) cornstarch

1 ¾ cups (414ml) heavy cream, divided

2 packets Duncan Hines Cotton Candy Frosting Creations™ Flavor Mix

⅔ cup (133g) sugar

⅛ teaspoon salt

6 Oreo cookies, broken into pieces

6 chocolate chip cookies, broken into pieces

Fill a large bowl with ice water. In a small bowl, combine 2 tablespoons (30ml) of the milk with the cornstarch, whisk and set aside. In another bowl, stir together ½ cup (118ml) of the cream and the flavor mix powder. Whisk vigorously to combine. Combine the remaining milk with the remaining 1 ¼ cups (296ml) heavy cream and sugar in a medium saucepan and place over medium heat. Bring the milk mixture to a low boil. Cook until the sugar dissolves, 3 minutes.

Remove the milk mixture from the heat and gradually whisk in the cornstarch mixture. Return to a boil and cook over moderately high heat until the mixture is slightly thickened, about 1 minute. Gradually pour the hot milk mixture into the bowl with the cream/flavor mix mixture. Whisk in the salt. Set the bowl in the ice water bath to cool, 20 minutes, whisking occasionally. Cover and refrigerate until well chilled, at least 4 hours or overnight.

Once chilled, pour the ice cream base into an ice cream maker and churn according to the manufacturer's instructions. When the ice cream has finished churning, gently fold in the cookie pieces. Pack the ice cream into a freezer-safe container. Freeze until firm, at least 4 hours.

THE MOUNTAINS OF MILK AND CREAM

Arizona, Colorado, Idaho, Montana, Nevada, New Mexico, Utah, Wyoming

The Mountain region is not all that it seems. For one, it is not entirely made up of mountains. The salt flats of Utah, the arid deserts of Nevada and the red rocks of Arizona are proof of the varied landscape. Each part holds its own beauty. The Mountain region is full of spirit from its people and its land, and some say it possesses magical powers.

The ice creams from the Mountain region are also not what they would seem. Some flavors are inspired by the spirit of the region, such as Chipotle Raspberry from Wyoming or Huckleberry from Montana, while other flavors are as unique as the landscape, such as Café Olé from New Mexico and Plum Lemon Verbena from Arizona. Try the flavors in this chapter and experience something truly magical.

Colorado Sour Cherry Ice Cream
Sweet Action Ice Cream, Denver, Colorado

MAKES 1 ½ QUARTS (1.4L)

Inspired by the vibrant red sour cherries grown on the western slopes of Colorado, this flavor packs a punch with elements of tart, sweet and tangy. Sweet Action creates ice creams made with fresh and seasonal ingredients, so the owners only feature this gem of a flavor on their menu when cherries are at their peak season. Lucky for you, they have chosen to share their recipe so you can make this ice cream whenever cherries are in season near your home.

3 cups (465g) sour cherries, pitted

1 ¼ cups (250g) sugar, divided

1 tbsp (15ml) lemon juice

2 cups (473ml) heavy cream

1 cup (237ml) whole milk

Combine cherries with ¾ cup (150g) of the sugar and lemon juice. Allow the cherries to macerate in the refridgerator for approximately 6 hours, stirring every hour. Purée the macerated cherries in a blender. Strain through a fine-mesh sieve to remove the cherry skins; reserve the juice. Reserve 2 tablespoons (30g) of the cherry skins and discard the remaining skins.

Fill a large bowl with ice water and set aside. Combine the remaining ½ cup (100g) sugar with the heavy cream and whole milk and place over medium heat. Bring the milk mixture to a low boil. Cook until the sugar dissolves, 3 minutes. Remove from the heat, transfer to a medium bowl and set in the ice water bath to cool, 20 minutes, whisking occasionally. Cover and refrigerate until well chilled, at least 4 hours or overnight.

When you are ready to churn, combine the reserved sour cherry juice and the milk mixture in an ice cream maker and churn according to the manufacturer's instructions. When churning is near completion, add the reserved cherry skins (adjust based on personal preference). Complete churning, transfer to a freezer-safe container and freeze until firm, at least 4 hours.

Note: If you cannot find sour or tart cherries, you may substitute sweet cherries. To prepare the cherries, pit and halve before macerating. Add ½ teaspoon citric acid during maceration. The ice cream will not taste exactly the same, but it will still be tart and delicious.

Sweet Action
ice cream

Café Olé Ice Cream

Adapted from recipe by Taos Cow Ice Cream Co., Arroyo Seco, New Mexico

MAKES 1 QUART (940ML)

As a play on the beverage café au lait, Café Olé is a spiced-up version of coffee ice cream with some fiery attitude. The flavor is a favorite of owner Jamie Leeson, as he is originally from Rhode Island where coffee milk and coffee cabinets are a religion. His customers love the flavor as well, and his wife frequently tells the story that she fell in love with him over this flavor. Café Olé is so popular that it has been copied many times by restaurants in New Mexico, but they are never as good as the original. Now you can get in on the secret to making this spicy coffee scoop.

6 egg yolks

1 ½ cups (355ml) 2% milk

½ cup (100g) packed brown sugar

Pinch of salt

1 ½ cups (135g) whole coffee beans, light to medium roast

1 ½ cups (355ml) heavy cream

½ tsp vanilla extract

3 ½ oz (98g) dark chocolate

½ tsp ground cinnamon

Pinch of red chile powder (optional)

Lightly whisk the egg yolks in a medium bowl and set aside. Combine the milk, brown sugar, salt and coffee beans in a medium saucepan. Cook over medium heat until bubbles begin to form. Remove from the heat, cover and steep for 1 hour. Strain the mixture through a sieve into a medium bowl; Discard the coffee beans. Add the cream and stir to combine.

Return the ice cream base to the saucepan. Warm over medium heat until the mixture is hot and begins to bubble, 3 to 4 minutes. Turn off the heat. Temper the eggs by slowly pouring ½ cup (118ml) of the warmed coffee-infused milk mixture into the yolks, whisking constantly until combined. Return the warmed yolks to the pan with the remaining milk mixture. Heat the custard over medium-low heat, stirring constantly, until the custard thickens and coats the back of a spoon. Remove from the heat and pour through a fine-mesh sieve into a medium bowl. Cool to room temperature and add the vanilla. Cover and refrigerate until well chilled, at least 4 hours or overnight.

Break up the dark chocolate and melt in a double boiler. Once the chocolate is melted, add the cinnamon and red chile powder (if desired). Whisk until smooth. Pour and spread evenly on a parchment paper–lined baking sheet or silicone mat and freeze.

When the base is thoroughly chilled, pour into an ice cream maker and churn according to the manufacturer's instructions. Roughly chop the frozen chocolate. When the ice cream is finished churning, gently fold in the chocolate pieces. Transfer to a freezer-safe container and freeze until firm, at least 4 hours. Eat fresh to avoid ice crystals.

Plum Lemon Verbena Ice Cream
Sweet Republic Artisan Ice Cream, Scottsdale, Arizona

MAKES 1 ½ QUARTS (1.4L)

The soothing yet robust flavor of lemon verbena is a favorite of owner Helen Yung. When her friend shared some of the herb from her garden, it inspired Helen to use it in ice cream. Looking to bring some fruity flavor contrast to the ice cream, Helen added Santa Rosa plums from a local farm. These plums are small in size but giant in flavor and they give the ice cream a lovely pink hue. The customer response has been wonderful. Helen hopes you enjoy this light and flavorful seasonal treat.

¾ lb (340g) Santa Rosa or other local plums, pitted and cut into quarters

1 cup (200g) sugar, divided

1 large egg yolk

2 tbsp (15g) nonfat dry milk

1 ¼ cups (295ml) whole milk

¾ cup (177ml) heavy cream

½ cup fresh lemon verbena leaves (or 2 tbsp dried leaves)

Combine the pitted plums with ¼ cup (50g) of the sugar in a saucepan. Cook over medium heat, stirring frequently, until soft, about 15 minutes. Cool slightly. Purée in a blender until smooth. Refrigerate until chilled.

Fill a large bowl with ice water. Whisk the egg yolk and 2 tablespoons (25g) sugar in a medium bowl until pale in color and set aside. Whisk together the remaining sugar and nonfat dry milk in a nonreactive saucepan. Gradually whisk in the whole milk until no lumps remain. Add the cream and whisk to combine.

Place the saucepan with the milk mixture over medium heat. Gently crush the verbena leaves by hand and sprinkle into the pan. When the mixture reaches a simmer, slowly pour 1 cup (237ml) of the warmed milk mixture into the yolks, whisking constantly until combined. Return the warmed yolks to the pan with the remaining milk mixture. Heat the custard over medium-low heat, stirring constantly, until the custard thickens and coats the back of a spoon, leaving a clear line. Remove from the heat and pour through a fine-mesh sieve into a medium bowl, pressing on the lemon verbena leaves with a spoon to extract all the flavor. Set the bowl in the ice water bath to cool, 20 minutes, whisking occasionally. Cover and refrigerate until well chilled, at least 4 hours or overnight.

Once chilled, combine the ice cream base and plum mixture, stirring to completely incorporate. Churn in an ice cream maker according to the manufacturer's instructions. Transfer to a freezer-safe container and freeze for at least 4 hours.

Huckleberry Ice Cream
Sweet Peaks Homemade Ice Cream, Whitefish, Montana

MAKES 1 QUART (940ML)

Huckleberries are a favorite fruit in Montana. They grow wild in the higher elevations and are enjoyed by humans and animals alike. Montanans love their huckleberries, staking out patches in the woods for gathering during "Huck season." At Sweet Peaks, huckleberry is the most popular flavor. Tourists to Montana feel compelled to order the ice cream for a true Montana experience while the local ice cream eaters are just simply wild about this little fruit—especially when churned into ice cream.

½ tsp tapioca starch

1 tsp water

1 cup (150g) huckleberries, fresh or frozen

1 cup (200g) sugar

4 large egg yolks

½ cup (118ml) whole milk

1 ½ cups (355ml) heavy cream

Whisk the tapioca starch and water in a small bowl and set aside. Combine the huckleberries and sugar in a small saucepan. Warm over medium heat, stirring frequently, until the mixture is simmering, slightly reduced and the berries begin to release their juices, 8 to 10 minutes. Remove from the heat and add the tapioca starch mixture, whisking until combined. Return to low heat and warm until slightly thickened. Remove from the heat and set aside.

Fill a large bowl with ice water and set aside. Lightly whisk the egg yolks in a medium bowl and set aside. Combine the milk and cream in a medium saucepan and warm over medium heat until the mixture is hot and begins to bubble. Reduce the heat to low and simmer for 3 minutes. Temper the eggs by slowly pouring ½ cup (118ml) of the warmed cream mixture into the yolks, whisking constantly until combined. Return the warmed yolks to the pan with the remaining cream mixture. Heat the custard over medium-low heat, stirring constantly, until the custard thickens and coats the back of a spoon, 1 to 2 minutes. Remove from the heat and pour through a fine-mesh sieve into a medium bowl. Set the bowl in the ice water bath to cool, 20 minutes, whisking occasionally.

Combine the huckleberry/sugar mixture and cooled custard in a blender and blend until the huckleberries are fully incorporated and the berry bits are broken apart. Cover and refrigerate until well chilled, at least 4 hours or overnight.

Once chilled, pour the ice cream base into an ice cream maker and churn according to the manufacturer's instructions. Transfer to a freezer-safe container and freeze until firm, at least 4 hours.

Tip: If Huck season does not happen in your area, substitute fresh or frozen blueberries for the huckleberries in this recipe. Frozen wild huckleberries are also available online.

Batter's Up Ice Cream
Inspired by Susie Scoops Ice Cream, Incline Village, Nevada

MAKES 1 QUART (940ML)

Food memories are some of the strongest memories we experience: so many people gravitate toward ice cream flavors that remind them of childhood, fun times with good company or a favorite vacation. Susie Scoops is a favorite ice cream destination for locals and visitors to the Lake Tahoe area. Customers visit year-round to enjoy their favorite flavors. Batter's Up, with its creamy cake batter ice cream swirled with ribbons of dark chocolate fudge, is an ice cream both children and adults enjoy.

ICE CREAM BASE

1 ¾ cups (414ml) whole milk

1 ½ cups (355ml) heavy cream

⅔ cup (133g) sugar

⅔ cup (60g) yellow cake mix

⅛ tsp salt

CHOCOLATE SAUCE

¼ cup (50g) sugar

3 tbsp (45ml) light corn syrup

½ cup (118ml) water

2 tbsp (14g) cocoa powder

¼ teaspoon vanilla extract

3 oz (84g) bittersweet chocolate, finely chopped

To make the ice cream base, fill a large bowl with ice water. Combine the milk, heavy cream and sugar in a medium saucepan and place over medium heat. Bring the milk mixture to a low boil. Cook until the sugar dissolves, 3 minutes. Pour into a medium bowl. Whisk in the cake mix and salt. Set the bowl in the ice water bath to cool, 20 minutes, whisking occasionally. Cover and refrigerate until well chilled, at least 4 hours or overnight.

To make the chocolate sauce, whisk together the sugar, corn syrup and water in a medium saucepan. Warm over medium heat, whisking frequently, until the mixture comes to a boil. Cook for 1 minute, whisking frequently until the sugar dissolves. Remove from the heat, whisk in the cocoa powder, then stir in the vanilla and continue whisking until smooth. Add the chocolate, let sit for 2 minutes and then stir well. Chill completely before swirling in the ice cream.

Once the ice cream base is chilled, whisk and pour it into an ice cream maker. Churn according to the manufacturer's instructions. Spoon a small layer of chocolate sauce into a freezer-safe container and lightly spoon a layer of ice cream on top. Continue to alternate layers of sauce and ice cream until the container is full, gently swirling with a spoon (careful not to muddy the ice cream). Freeze until firm, at least 4 hours.

Le'lemon Berry Ice Cream
Inspired by CloverLeaf Creamery, Buhl, Idaho

MAKES 1 QUART (940ML)

Each year, CloverLeaf Creamery participates in a community fundraiser day. Businesses from around the town submit flavor ideas to be made by the creamery and judged by the crowds. Le'lemon Berry—tart lemon ice cream swirled with sweet strawberries and chunks of white chocolate—was the winning flavor in the 2012 contest and is now produced full time by the creamery. If you are looking for a refreshing ice cream, try this blue ribbon scoop.

STRAWBERRY SWIRL

2 cups (473ml) mashed strawberries

½ cup (100g) sugar

¼ tsp vanilla extract

LEMON SYRUP

3 or 4 lemons

2 tbsp (25g) sugar

ICE CREAM BASE

1 ½ cups (355ml) whole milk, divided

1 tbsp (9g) cornstarch

1 ¾ cups (414ml) heavy cream

⅔ cup (133g) sugar

⅛ tsp salt

½ cup (90g) white chocolate chips, chopped (optional for added sweetness and crunch)

First, combine the strawberries and sugar in a medium saucepan. Stir until the berries begin to macerate. Place over medium-low heat. Cook, stirring occasionally, until the strawberries are broken down, 5 to 8 minutes. Reduce the heat to low and simmer until the mixture is reduced by half of its original volume, 10 minutes. Remove from the heat and cool to room temperature. Stir in the vanilla. Cover and chill completely.

To prepare the lemon syrup, use a vegetable peeler to remove the zest of 2 lemons in large strips; set aside. Squeeze the lemons until you have ½ cup (118ml) of juice. Combine the juice with the sugar in a small saucepan and place over medium heat. Heat until the sugar is dissolved, 1 to 2 minutes. Pour into a small bowl, cover and refrigerate until completely cool.

To make the ice cream base, fill a large bowl with ice water. In a small bowl, combine 2 tablespoons (30ml) of the milk with the cornstarch, whisk and set aside. Combine the remaining milk with the heavy cream, sugar and reserved lemon zest in a medium saucepan and place over medium heat. Bring the milk mixture to a low boil. Cook until the sugar dissolves, 3 minutes.

Remove the milk mixture from the heat and gradually whisk in the cornstarch mixture. Return to a boil and cook over moderately high heat until the mixture is slightly thickened, about 1 minute. Pour into a medium bowl. Whisk in the salt. Set the bowl in the ice water bath to cool, 20 minutes, whisking occasionally. Cover and refrigerate until well chilled, at least 4 hours or overnight.

Once ice cream base is chilled, remove the zest with a slotted spoon. Add the lemon syrup and stir to combine. Pour into an ice cream maker and churn according to the manufacturer's instructions. When churning is complete, gently fold in the white chocolate pieces, if desired. Spoon a small layer of strawberry swirl into a freezer-safe container and lightly spoon a layer of ice cream on top. Continue to alternate layers of strawberry swirl and ice cream until the container is full. Freeze until firm, at least 4 hours.

Chipotle Raspberry Ice Cream
Inspired by the Ice Cream Café, Gillette, Wyoming

MAKES 1 QUART (940ML)

During holidays and special occasions, the McClure family always serves their favorite hors d'oeuvre of chipotle raspberry sauce spread over cream cheese and crackers. The ingredients in their favorite snack inspired the Ice Cream Café owners to try adding the unique flavor to vanilla ice cream. Eating a scoop of this ice cream starts with a sweet vanilla flavor, but just as your taste buds settle into the sweetness the spicy chipotle hits them with a bang! An acquired taste that spice lovers will be sure to enjoy.

CHIPOTLE RASPBERRY SAUCE

1 tbsp (15ml) olive oil

1 jalapeño pepper, seeded and minced

1 clove garlic, minced

1 chipotle pepper in adobo sauce, minced

1 tsp (5ml) adobo sauce

8 oz (227g) fresh raspberries

¼ cup (59ml) apple cider vinegar

½ tsp salt

2 tbsp (30ml) honey

3 tbsp (37g) brown sugar

ICE CREAM BASE

2 egg yolks

1 ¾ cups (414ml) heavy cream

1 ¾ cups (414ml) whole milk

⅔ cup (133g) granulated sugar

¼ tsp vanilla extract

To prepare the sauce, heat the olive oil in a medium skillet over medium heat. Add the jalapeño and cook until tender, 3 minutes. Add the garlic, chipotle pepper and adobo sauce, and cook for 1 minute. Stir in the raspberries and cook until the berries soften, 3 minutes. Add the vinegar, salt, honey and brown sugar. Bring to a boil, reduce the heat and simmer until thickened and reduced by half, about 15 minutes. Pour into a food processor and cool for 5 minutes. Purée until smooth. Cover and cool completely in the refrigerator before adding to the ice cream.

To make the ice cream base, fill a large bowl with ice water. Whisk the egg yolks in a small bowl and set aside. Combine the cream, milk and granulated sugar in a medium saucepan and warm over medium heat until the mixture is hot and the sugar dissolves, 4 to 5 minutes. Temper the eggs by slowly pouring ½ cup (118ml) of the warmed cream mixture into the yolks, whisking constantly until combined. Return the warmed yolks to the pan with the remaining cream mixture. Heat the custard over medium-low heat, stirring constantly, until the custard thickens and coats the back of a spoon. Remove from the heat and pour through a fine-mesh sieve into a medium bowl. Set the bowl in the ice water bath to cool, 20 minutes, whisking occasionally. Add the vanilla and stir to combine. Cover and refrigerate until well chilled, at least 4 hours or overnight.

Once chilled, pour the ice cream base into an ice cream maker and churn according to the manufacturer's instructions. Spoon a small layer of chipotle raspberry sauce into a freezer-safe container and lightly spoon a layer of ice cream on top. Continue to alternate layers of sauce and ice cream until the container is full, gently swirling with a spoon (careful not to muddy the ice cream). Freeze until firm, at least 4 hours.

Lemongrass Gelato
Inspired by Dolcetti Gelato, Salt Lake City, Utah

MAKES 1 QUART (940ML)

Dolcetti owners Elizabeth and Mark England love to travel the world. While traveling in Thailand, they grew to love the subtle combinations of ingredients found in the food of the country. When they returned home, the Englands created a gelato to remember the trip. This recipe is a combination of favorite flavors used in Thai cooking. Lemongrass has a bright and earthy flavor while coconut cream gives the gelato a wonderfully smooth texture. The Englands are artists in addition to gelato makers, and their creativity shines through this exciting recipe.

One 14-oz (473ml) can coconut cream

1 ¾ cups (411ml) whole milk

½ cup (118ml) heavy cream

¾ cup (150g) sugar

Four 4" (10cm) stalks lemongrass, finely chopped

Combine all the ingredients in a medium saucepan. Place over medium heat and warm until the mixture is hot and steam begins rise, 4 to 5 minutes. Remove from the heat, cover and let steep at room temperature for 1 hour. Pour the mixture into a medium bowl. Cover and refrigerate overnight.

Once chilled, pour the mixture through a fine-mesh sieve into a medium bowl. Discard the lemongrass. Pour the ice cream base into an ice cream maker and churn according to the manufacturer's instructions. Transfer to a freezer-safe container and freeze until firm, at least 4 hours.

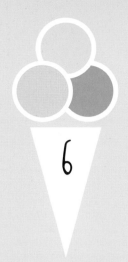

THE WILD WILD WEST

Alaska, California, Hawaii, Oregon, Washington

If you have made it this far in the cookbook, you have traveled coast to coast through the varied regions of the United States, finding unique and flavorful ice creams along the way. The West is no exception.

California is home to some of the most intriguing ice creams in the country, influenced by the melting pot of cultures and inspiring flavors, such as Mango and Avocado Lime. Heading north to Oregon, you will find distinctive ice creams, such as Brown Sugar Sour Cream, tucked in between the rocky coast and beautiful gorges. Washington is the gem of the Pacific Northwest and home to clear water, snowy peaks and exceptional ice cream flavors like Mayan Chocolate. Alaska and Hawaii, with their sweeping natural beauty, inspire flavors such as Arctic Refuge Wild Berry Snap and Green Tea.

Finish up your tour of the best ice cream parlors in the United States by experiencing some wild ice cream flavors found only in the West.

Mango Ice Cream
Mitchell's Ice Cream, San Francisco, California

MAKES ABOUT 1 ½ QUARTS (1.4L)

Mango has been the number one selling flavor at Mitchell's for over 50 years. Owner Larry Mitchell started importing mangoes in the 1960s at the suggestion of a customer who imported fruit from the Philippines. The flavor became an instant hit, attracting many of the neighborhood immigrants from Mexico, Central America and the Philippines. Mango reminded these customers of home and they began to request other fruit flavors that they loved and missed. Mitchell's began importing other exotic fruits, one at a time, and soon the store had a reputation for having unusual tropical flavors, which it still produces to this day.

4 small to medium ripe mangoes*

2 pasteurized eggs (see instructions if using unpasteurized eggs)

1 cup (200g) cane sugar

1 tbsp (15ml) fresh lemon juice

2 cups (473ml) heavy cream

¼ cup (59ml) whole milk

Peel, pit and slice the mangoes and purée in a blender or food processor. Set aside 1 ½ cups (355ml) of mango purée, reserving the remaining purée for other delicious uses. If the mangoes seem fibrous, pass the purée through a sieve to remove excess fibers.

Whisk the eggs in a medium bowl until pale in color, about 2 minutes. When they become thick, add the sugar and continue to whisk. Add the lemon juice, cream and milk and whisk until combined. *If you are using eggs that are not pasteurized, pour the entire mixture into a saucepan and warm over medium heat, stirring constantly, until warm and steam starts to form. Cool to room temperature.* Cover and refrigerate until well chilled, at least 2 hours.

Once chilled, pour the ice cream base into an ice cream maker and churn according to the manufacturer's instructions. Transfer to a freezer-safe container and freeze until firm, at least 4 hours.

* Mitchell's prefers to use Manila mangoes (imported from the Philippines). They also suggest using Ataulfo mangoes (from Mexico). These varieties are sweet and not fibrous. If you cannot find these varieties, be sure to strain your purée to remove fibers and taste your base as you go, adding more sugar if needed.

Brown Sugar Sour Cream Ice Cream
Adapted from recipe by Ruby Jewel Ice Cream, Portland, Oregon

MAKES 1 QUART (940ML)

Ruby Jewel co-owner Lisa Herlinger-Esco was inspired to create this flavor by her love of dipping fresh strawberries into sour cream and brown sugar. Laced with the sweet molasses character of brown sugar and the tang of sour cream, this ice cream pairs well with any fruit as well as a streusel, granola or nut topping. It is a perfect dessert for sweet summer nights.

2 tbsp (29g) unsalted butter

½ cup (100g) packed dark brown sugar

1 ½ tsp (7.5ml) water

⅓ cup (79ml) sour cream

Pinch of salt

2 egg yolks

1 ¾ cups (414ml) heavy cream

1 ¾ cups (414ml) whole milk

¼ cup (50g) granulated sugar

⅛ tsp vanilla extract

Combine the butter, brown sugar and water in a small saucepan and place over medium-low heat. Warm until the butter and sugar are melted, about 2 minutes. Remove from the heat and pour into a medium bowl. Cool for 5 minutes. Add the sour cream and salt, whisking to combine. Place a fine-mesh sieve over the bowl and set aside.

Fill a large bowl with ice water. Whisk the egg yolks in a small bowl and set aside. In a medium saucepan, combine the cream, milk and granulated sugar. Warm over medium heat until the mixture is hot and the sugar dissolves, 4 to 5 minutes. Temper the eggs by slowly pouring ½ cup (118ml) of the warmed cream mixture into the yolks, whisking constantly until combined. Return the warmed yolks to the pan with the remaining cream mixture. Heat the custard over medium-low heat, stirring constantly, until the custard thickens and coats the back of a spoon. Remove from the heat and pour through the fine-mesh sieve into the sour cream mixture. Whisk thoroughly. Set the bowl in the ice water bath to cool, 20 minutes, whisking occasionally. Add the vanilla. Cover and refrigerate until well chilled, at least 4 hours or overnight.

Once chilled, pour the ice cream base into an ice cream maker and churn according to the manufacturer's instructions. Transfer to a freezer-safe container and freeze until firm, at least 4 hours.

Green Tea Ice Cream
Inspired by Dave's Hawaiian Ice Cream, Oahu, Hawaii

MAKES 1 QUART (940ML)

Green tea originated in China and has been associated with many cultures throughout Asia. It was introduced to Hawaiian culture when sugar plantation workers arrived in the early 1800s, bringing many Asian-influenced flavors to the islands. Green tea is now popular all over the world, but many Hawaiians feel like it is an integral part of their culture. Dave's Hawaiian Ice Cream shares their love of green tea through this soothing ice cream flavor.

1 ½ cups (355ml) whole milk, divided

1 tbsp (9g) cornstarch

1 ¾ cups (414ml) heavy cream, divided

2 tbsp (16g) matcha powder

⅔ cup (133g) sugar

⅛ teaspoon salt

Fill a large bowl with ice water. In a small bowl, combine 2 tablespoons (30ml) of the milk with the cornstarch, whisk and set aside. In another bowl, add ½ cup (118ml) of the cream and matcha powder. Whisk vigorously to combine.

Combine the remaining milk with the remaining 1 ¼ cups (296ml) heavy cream and sugar in a medium saucepan. Place over medium heat and bring the milk mixture to a low boil. Cook until the sugar dissolves, 3 minutes.

Remove the milk mixture from the heat and gradually whisk in the cornstarch mixture. Return to a boil and cook over moderately high heat until the mixture is slightly thickened, about 1 minute. Gradually pour the hot milk mixture into the bowl with the cream/matcha mixture. Whisk in the salt. Set the bowl in the ice water bath to cool, 20 minutes, whisking occasionally. Cover and refrigerate until well chilled, at least 4 hours or overnight.

Once chilled, pour the ice cream base into an ice cream maker and churn according to the manufacturer's instructions. Transfer to a freezer-safe container and freeze until firm, at least 4 hours.

Note: Matcha is finely milled green tea. It is bright green and a very fine powder. Matcha can be found in the tea aisle of most grocery stores, or look for it at your local Asian market.

Arctic Refuge Wild Berry Snap Ice Cream

Adapted from recipe by Hot Licks Homemade Ice Cream, Fairbanks, Alaska

MAKES 1 GENEROUS QUART (940ML)

Hot Licks showcases several ice cream flavors inspired by the elegance of the Alaskan wilderness, including this delicious creamy, tart and spicy creation, which was developed in cooperation with the Northern Alaska Environmental Center to honor the Arctic National Wildlife Refuge.

2 egg yolks

1 ¾ cups (414ml) heavy cream

1 ¾ cups (414ml) whole milk

⅔ cup + 5 tbsp (193g) sugar, divided

Pinch of salt

1 tsp vanilla extract

½ cup (96g) fresh or frozen blueberries

½ cup (65g) fresh or frozen cranberries

1 tbsp (15ml) water

½ cup (30g) crumbled gingersnaps

Fill a large bowl with ice water. Whisk the egg yolks in a medium bowl and set aside. Combine the cream, milk, ⅔ cup (133g) sugar and pinch of salt in a medium saucepan. Warm over medium heat until the mixture is hot and the sugar dissolves, 4 to 5 minutes. Temper the eggs by slowly pouring ½ cup (118ml) of the warmed cream mixture into the yolks, whisking constantly until combined. Return the warmed yolks to the pan with the remaining cream mixture. Heat the custard over medium-low heat, stirring constantly, until the custard thickens and coats the back of a spoon. Remove from the heat and pour through a fine-mesh sieve into a medium bowl. Set the bowl in the ice water bath to cool, 20 minutes, whisking occasionally. Add the vanilla. Cover and refrigerate until well chilled, at least 4 hours or overnight.

To prepare a blueberry swirl, combine the blueberries and 2 tablespoons (25g) sugar in a small saucepan and place over medium heat. Stir constantly until the blueberries begin to burst, about 5 minutes. Turn the heat to low and simmer, stirring frequently, until the blueberries break down and release all of their juice, 2 minutes. Remove from the heat and cool completely.

To prepare a cranberry swirl, combine the cranberries and remaining 3 tablespoons (37g) sugar in a small saucepan and place over medium heat. Stir constantly until the cranberries begin to burst, about 5 minutes. Turn the heat to low and simmer, stirring frequently, until the cranberries break down and release all of their juice, 3 to 5 minutes. Add the water and stir to combine. Remove from the heat and cool completely.

Once chilled, pour the ice cream base into an ice cream maker and churn according to the manufacturer's instructions. Sprinkle a layer of gingersnaps into a freezer-safe container and drizzle with a small layer of blueberry and cranberry swirl. Lightly spoon a layer of ice cream on top. Continue to alternate layers of cookies and swirl and ice cream until the container is full, *gently* swirling with a spoon (careful not to muddy the ice cream). Freeze until firm, at least 4 hours.

Mayan Chocolate Ice Cream
Full Tilt Ice Cream, Seattle, Washington

MAKES ABOUT 1 QUART (940ML)

Ice cream shop owners cater to a wide variety of food and flavor preferences. It is important for the nondairy-eating public to enjoy the ice cream experience as much as the dairy-loving ice cream eater. Full Tilt, as well as many other ice cream shops around the country, is producing creative vegan ice creams made with nondairy milks such as coconut milk, almond milk and rice milk. The creamy combination of coconut milk and spices in this chocolate vegan ice cream is a spicy and refreshing scoop for all to enjoy.

3 ½ cups (790ml) regular coconut milk

¾ cup (150g) sugar

½ tsp ground cinnamon

⅛ tsp ground ginger

⅛ tsp ground cardamom

¼ cup (28g) Dutch cocoa powder

Warm the coconut milk in a saucepan over medium-low heat. Whisk in the sugar, cinnamon, ginger and cardamom. Continue to heat the mixture over medium-low heat until the sugar is dissolved, about 5 minutes. Remove from the heat and whisk in the cocoa powder. Use an immersion blender or an upright blender to purée the mixture until smooth and no lumps of cocoa powder remain. Pour into a medium bowl, cover and refrigerate overnight.

Once chilled, pour the ice cream base into an ice cream maker and churn according to the manufacturer's instructions. Transfer to a freezer-safe container and freeze until firm, at least 4 hours.

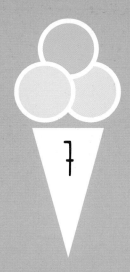

INSPIRATIONS FROM MY ICE CREAM TRAVELS

Throughout my search for the best ice cream recipes in the country, I was constantly inspired by unique flavor ideas. Discussions with ice cream shop owners sparked new ideas for my own ice cream making adventures. My home region of the Southeast inspired comfort flavors such as Peanut Butter and Jelly and Cranberry Walnut. The South and its decadent sweets inspired flavors like Red Velvet and King Cake.

One good ice cream idea often leads to another, such as the flavor Buttered Almond to be paired with Popcorn Ice Cream from the Northeast. The Mountain region, with its wooded mountains and red rocks, inspired the fresh flavors of Rosemary Honey Walnut and Prickly Pear Coconut. The fertile lands of the West provided inspiration for several fruity scoops, including Goat Cheese Ice Cream with Pickled Blueberries and Spiced Strawberry Rhubarb Swirl.

This final cookbook chapter is filled with exciting ice cream flavors inspired by the regions of the United States and their fantastic array of ice creams. Read through this chapter and you may just find some inspiration of your own.

Fennel Ice Cream with Blood Orange Sauce

MAKES 1 QUART (940ML)

Basil is not the only herb that can be the star of a scoop of ice cream. Fennel, with its wonderful anise quality, becomes an elegant starlet with the addition of some cream and sugar. Bursting with fragrance and flavor, this ice cream will knock your socks off with the addition of a tart blood orange sauce. Served as an intriguing ending to a fancy meal or as snack on the couch, this ice cream is sure to please to the palate.

ICE CREAM BASE

1 ½ cups (355ml) whole milk, divided

1 ¾ cups (414ml) heavy cream

⅔ cup (133g) sugar

1 tbsp (5g) fennel seeds

1 tbsp (9g) cornstarch

⅛ tsp salt

BLOOD ORANGE SAUCE

1 cup (237ml) blood orange juice

⅓ cup (67g) sugar

To make the ice cream base, combine 1 cup (237ml) of the milk, cream, sugar and fennel seeds in a medium saucepan and place over medium-high heat. Once the mixture is hot and steam begins rise, remove from the heat, cover and let steep at room temperature for 1 hour. When steeping is almost complete, fill a large bowl with ice water. In a small bowl, combine 2 tablespoons (30ml) milk with the cornstarch, whisk and set aside.

When steeping is complete, pour the milk mixture through a fine-mesh sieve to remove the fennel seeds. Return the milk mixture to the saucepan and add the remaining 6 tablespoons (90ml) milk. Place over medium heat and bring the milk mixture to a low boil. Cook for 3 minutes.

Remove the milk mixture from the heat and gradually whisk in the cornstarch mixture. Return to a boil and cook over moderately high heat until the mixture is slightly thickened, about 1 minute. Pour into a medium bowl and whisk in the salt. Set the bowl in the ice water bath to cool, 20 minutes, whisking occasionally. Cover and chill overnight.

To make the blood orange sauce, combine the blood orange juice and sugar in a small saucepan and place over medium heat. Bring to a simmer, stirring occasionally, until the sugar is dissolved, 1 to 2 minutes. Continue to simmer until the sauce is reduced by half of its volume (about ½ cup [118ml]), 10 to 12 minutes. Remove from the heat and cool completely in the refrigerator before serving with the ice cream.

Once the ice cream base is chilled, pour it into an ice cream maker and churn according to the manufacturer's instructions. Transfer to a freezer-safe container and freeze until firm, at least 4 hours. Serve with a generous drizzle of blood orange sauce.

Buttered Almond Ice Cream

MAKES 1 QUART (940ML)

Do you prefer butter with your popcorn? Salty, crunchy and sweet is a combination of flavors and textures that few people can turn down, but add the unctuous quality of butter and you are in for a real treat. Pair this sweet, salty, crunchy and buttery ice cream with Popcorn Ice Cream (page 60) and you will have the ultimate movie treat, not to mention being the envy of everyone around you.

ICE CREAM BASE

1 ½ cups (355ml) whole milk, divided

1 tbsp (9g) cornstarch

¾ lb (340g) unsalted butter

1 ¾ cups (414ml) heavy cream

⅔ cup (133g) sugar

⅛ tsp salt

¾ cup (128g) buttered almonds (see below)

BUTTERED ALMONDS

¾ cup (128g) roasted, unsalted almonds,

1 tbsp (14g) unsalted butter, melted

½ tsp salt

To make the ice cream base, fill a large bowl with ice water. In a small bowl, combine 2 tablespoons (30ml) of the milk with the cornstarch, whisk and set aside. Place the butter in a medium saucepan and melt over medium heat. Bring the butter to a boil and simmer until the foam subsides but the butter has not yet browned, about 5 minutes. Remove from the heat and let stand for a few minutes, allowing the butter solids to settle to the bottom of the pan. Slowly pour the clarified butter into a container. When there is very little oil remaining, use a small spoon to remove as much melted butter as possible. There should be about 1 tablespoon (14g) of butter solids and a small bit of melted butter remaining. Store clarified butter for future use.

Add the remaining milk, heavy cream and sugar to the butter solids and place over medium heat. Bring the milk mixture to a low boil. Cook until the sugar dissolves, 3 minutes. Remove from the heat and gradually whisk in the cornstarch mixture. Return to a boil and cook over moderately high heat until the mixture is slightly thickened, about 1 minute. Remove from the heat and pour into a medium bowl. Whisk in the salt. Set the bowl in the ice water bath to cool, 20 minutes, whisking occasionally. Cover and chill overnight.

To make the buttered almonds, preheat the oven to 350°F (180°C, or gas mark 4). Combine all the ingredients in a medium bowl, tossing to coat the almonds. Spread the mixture evenly on a baking sheet and bake for 10 to 15 minutes, stirring once, until slightly toasted and aromatic. Let cool completely. Chop before adding to the ice cream.

Once chilled, pour the ice cream base into an ice cream maker and churn according to the manufacturer's instructions. When churning is complete, gently fold in most of the buttered almonds. Transfer to a freezer-safe container and finish with a sprinkle of remaining almonds. Freeze until firm, at least 4 hours.

Tip: Substitute smoked almonds for a slightly savory twist.

Pumpkin Ale Ice Cream

MAKES 1 QUART (940ML)

Fall is my favorite season. It brings cooler weather, comfort food, the smell of falling leaves and crisp air. Fall also brings pumpkins. Everywhere you turn, pumpkins are being used in food and decoration. There is one seasonal inspiration for which I never tire and that is pumpkin beer. Choose the right brew and you will find yourself drinking a flavorful ale full of fall spices and sweet pumpkin taste. This ice cream will provide you with the same comforting feeling and flavor.

½ cup (90g) canned unsweetened pumpkin purée

1 tsp vanilla extract

¼ tsp salt

1 ¾ cups (414ml) whole milk, divided

1 tbsp (9g) cornstarch

1 ½ cups (355ml) heavy cream

½ cup (100g) packed dark brown sugar

¼ cup (50g) granulated sugar

⅔ cup (158 ml) pumpkin ale, chilled

Spoon the canned pumpkin into a large piece of cheesecloth. Gather the cloth and squeeze over a small bowl, removing as much moisture as possible from the pumpkin. Transfer the pumpkin pulp to a blender. Add the vanilla and salt, pulse to combine and set aside.

Fill a large bowl with ice water. In a small bowl, combine 2 tablespoons (30ml) of the milk with the cornstarch, whisk and set aside. Combine the remaining milk with the heavy cream and sugars in a medium saucepan and place over medium heat. Bring the milk mixture to a low boil. Cook until the sugars dissolve, 3 minutes.

Remove the milk mixture from the heat and gradually whisk in the cornstarch mixture. Return to a boil and cook over moderately high heat until the mixture is slightly thickened, about 1 minute. Pour the milk mixture into the blender with the pumpkin mixture and purée until smooth. Pour into a medium bowl and set the bowl in the ice water bath to cool, 20 minutes, whisking occasionally. Cover and chill overnight.

Once chilled, add the pumpkin ale to the ice cream base and stir to combine. Pour into an ice cream maker and churn according to the manufacturer's instructions. Transfer to a freezer-safe container and freeze until firm, at least 4 hours.

Pistachio Rose Ice Cream

MAKES 1 QUART (940ML)

Although ice cream is a very popular frozen dessert in the United States, it is not always the most popular choice in other countries where different types of frozen desserts are produced. In India and neighboring countries, kulfi is a common frozen treat similar in appearance to ice cream yet denser because it is not churned. Pistachio and rose are popular kulfi flavors and are sometimes combined like the flavors in this scoop. Great culinary creations happen when cultures collide.

1 cup (124g) shelled unsalted pistachios

½ tsp salt

1 ½ cups (355ml) whole milk, divided

1 tbsp (9g) cornstarch

1 ¾ cups (414ml) heavy cream

⅔ cup (133g) sugar

1 tbsp (15ml) rosewater

Preheat the oven to 350°F (180°C, or gas mark 4). Spread the pistachios on a parchment- or silicone-lined rimmed baking sheet. Bake for 10 minutes, or until the nuts are toasted and fragrant, stirring halfway through baking. Remove from the oven and transfer ½ cup (62g) of the pistachios to a food processor. Purée until the pistachios resemble a smooth paste. Transfer to a medium bowl, add the salt and stir to combine. Cool the remaining ½ cup (62g) pistachios to room temperature and chop. Chill until ready to use.

Fill a large bowl with ice water. In a small bowl, combine 2 tablespoons (30ml) of the milk with the cornstarch, whisk and set aside. Combine the remaining milk with the heavy cream and sugar in a medium saucepan and place over medium heat. Bring the milk mixture to a low boil. Cook over moderate heat until the sugar dissolves, 3 minutes.

Remove the milk mixture from the heat and gradually whisk in the cornstarch mixture. Return to a boil and cook over moderately high heat until the mixture is slightly thickened, about 1 minute. Pour into the bowl with the pistachio paste and whisk to combine. Set the bowl in the ice water bath to cool, 20 minutes, whisking occasionally. Add the rosewater. Cover and refrigerate until well chilled, at least 4 hours or overnight.

Once chilled, pour the ice cream base into an ice cream maker and churn according to the manufacturer's instructions. When churning is complete, gently fold in the reserved pistachio pieces. Transfer to a freezer-safe container and freeze until firm, at least 4 hours.

Chocolate Sesame Brittle Ice Cream

MAKES 1 QUART (940ML)

Frequently used as an ingredient in savory dishes, sesame occassionally finds its way into sweets as well. The flavor combination of chocolate and nuts has always been a favorite of mine, so flavoring this chocolate ice cream with aromatic sesame was an easy choice. Sesame seeds bring a subtle yet delightful nuttiness to the ice cream while the sesame brittle gives the ice cream some sweet and salty crunch.

CHOCOLATE LIQUOR

½ cup (56g) cocoa powder

⅓ cup (79ml) water

¼ cup (50g) sugar

2 oz (56g) dark chocolate, chopped

⅓ cup (77g) tahini

ICE CREAM BASE

1 ½ cups (355ml) heavy cream, divided

1 ¾ cups (414ml) whole milk

½ cup (100g) sugar

½ tsp sea salt

½ tsp vanilla extract

1 cup chopped sesame brittle (see below)

SESAME BRITTLE

¼ cup (50g) sugar

2 tbsp (25g) brown sugar

2 tbsp (30ml) honey

⅛ tsp ground cinnamon

1 ½ tsp water

Pinch of salt

½ cup (80g) raw sesame seeds

½ tsp vanilla extract

2 tsp (10g) unsalted butter

⅛ teaspoon baking soda

To make the chocolate liquor, combine the cocoa powder, water and ¼ cup (50g) sugar in a small saucepan. Place the saucepan over medium heat and bring to a low boil, whisking constantly. As soon as bubbles form, remove from the heat and add the dark chocolate. Let sit for 2 minutes and then stir the chocolate liquor until smooth. Pour into a medium bowl, add the tahini and stir to combine.

To make the ice cream base, fill a large bowl with ice water. Combine ½ cup (118ml) of the cream, milk, ½ cup (100g) sugar and salt in a medium saucepan and place over medium heat. Bring to a low boil and cook until the sugar dissolves, 3 minutes. Remove from the heat and pour into the chocolate/tahini mixture, whisk to combine. Stir in remaining 1 cup (237ml) cream. Set the bowl in the ice water bath to cool, 20 minutes, whisking occasionally. Add the vanilla and stir to combine. Cover and refrigerate until well chilled, at least 4 hours or overnight.

To make the brittle, line a baking sheet with a silicone mat (if you do not have a silicone mat, leave the baking sheet ungreased). Combine the sugars, honey, cinnamon, water and salt in a small saucepan. Place over medium heat and warm, stirring frequently, until the ingredients are combined. Stir in the raw sesame seeds. Increase the heat to medium-high and cook the mixture, stirring frequently, until the mixture reaches 300°F (150°C) on a candy thermometer and turns an amber color, about 10 minutes.

When the sesame mixture reaches temperature, remove the pan from the heat and stir in the vanilla and butter. When the ingredients are combined, stir in the baking soda. Allow the mixture to sit and foam for 1 minute, stirring occasionally. Pour the mixture onto the prepared baking sheet (or directly onto the unprepared baking sheet). Allow the brittle to completely cool, 20 minutes, and then break into ½-inch (1.3cm) pieces.

Once the ice cream base is chilled, pour it into an ice cream maker and churn according to the manufacturer's instructions. When churning is complete, gently fold in the sesame brittle. Transfer to a freezer-safe container and freeze until firm, at least 4 hours.

Peanut Butter and Jelly Ice Cream

MAKES 1 GENEROUS QUART (940ML)

There is nothing more comforting than a simple and satisfying peanut butter and jelly sandwich. Creamy or crunchy, strawberry or grape, it does not matter. The end result is the same gratifying food experience. It seemed like common sense to make this familiar favorite into an ice cream flavor. With its creamy and salty peanut base and swirls of your favorite jam, this ice cream may just replace your go-to lunch.

1 ½ cups (355ml) whole milk, divided

1 tbsp (9g) cornstarch

½ cup (90g) unsalted natural peanut butter

½ teaspoon salt

1 ¾ cups (414ml) heavy cream

⅔ cup (133g) sugar

¾ cup (177ml) grape or strawberry jam

Fill a large bowl with ice water. In a small bowl, combine 2 tablespoons (30ml) of the milk with the cornstarch, whisk and set aside. Whisk the peanut butter and salt in a medium bowl and set aside.

Combine the remaining milk with the heavy cream and sugar in a medium saucepan and place over medium heat. Bring the milk mixture to a low boil. Cook until the sugar dissolves, 3 minutes. Remove from the heat and gradually whisk in the cornstarch mixture. Return to a boil and cook over moderately high heat until the mixture is slightly thickened, about 1 minute. Pour into the bowl with the peanut butter and whisk until smooth. Set the bowl in the ice water bath to cool, 20 minutes, whisking occasionally. Cover and refrigerate until well chilled, at least 4 hours or overnight.

Once chilled, pour the ice cream base into an ice cream maker and churn according to the manufacturer's instructions. Spoon a small layer of jam into a freezer-safe container and lightly spoon a layer of ice cream on top. Continue to alternate layers of jam and ice cream until the container is full, gently swirling with a spoon (careful not to muddy the ice cream). Freeze until firm, at least 4 hours.

Cranberry Walnut Ice Cream

MAKES 1 QUART (940ML)

Some of my favorite flavor creations are inspired by requests from family and friends. Requests arrive quite frequently at my doorstep. Cranberry Walnut was created after I received a request from my parents for an ice cream with fruit and nuts. The request came to me in the fall, so combining spicy cinnamon with sweet and tart cranberries and crunchy walnuts seemed seasonally appropriate. Every time I make this flavor my mother tells me it is amazing. It could be a mother's love or it could be that this flavor is just that darn good.

ICE CREAM BASE

1 ½ cups (355ml) whole milk, divided

1 ¾ cups (414ml) heavy cream

⅔ cup (133g) sugar

Ten 3" (7.5cm) cinnamon sticks

1 tbsp (9g) cornstarch

⅛ tsp salt

¼ cup (29g) chopped toasted walnuts

SOAKED CRANBERRIES

Cranberries can be prepared up to a day in advance.

2 tbsp (30ml) water

1 tbsp (12g) sugar

¼ cup (25g) dried unsweetened cranberries

1 tsp whiskey

To make the ice cream base, combine 1 cup (237ml) of the milk, cream, sugar and cinnamon sticks in a medium saucepan and place over medium-high heat. Warm until the mixture is hot and steam begins rise. Remove from the heat, cover and let steep at room temperature for 1 hour.

Fill a large bowl with ice water; set aside. In a small bowl, combine 2 tablespoons (30ml) milk with the cornstarch, whisk and set aside. When steeping is complete, remove the cinnamon sticks with a slotted spoon. Add the remaining milk and begin rewarming over medium heat. Bring the milk mixture to a low boil and cook for 3 minutes.

Remove the milk mixture from the heat and gradually whisk in the cornstarch mixture. Return to a boil and cook over moderately high heat until the mixture is slightly thickened, about 1 minute. Pour into a medium bowl and whisk in the salt. Set the bowl in the ice water bath to cool, 20 minutes, whisking occasionally. Cover and refrigerate until well chilled, at least 4 hours or overnight.

To make the soaked cranberries, heat the water and sugar in a small saucepan, stirring occasionally until the sugar is dissolved, 1 to 2 minutes. Add the cranberries and cook over low heat, stirring frequently, until all but about 1 tablespoon (15ml) of the syrup has been absorbed, about 5 minutes. Remove from the heat and add the whiskey. Cool completely before adding to the ice cream.

Once the ice cream base is chilled, pour it into an ice cream maker and churn according to the manufacturer's instructions. When churning is complete, gently fold in ¼ cup (25 g) of the soaked cranberries and walnuts. Transfer to a freezer-safe container and freeze until firm, at least 4 hours.

Breakfast of Champions

Occasionally we make bad food choices. Maybe it was the spicy food too close to bedtime, one too many bites from the buffet, or pizza and cake for breakfast. We are all guilty. But what about ice cream for breakfast? Try this ice cream and you will forget your bad decisions. Caramelized bananas and cornflakes flavor sweet cream just like they flavor the milk in your morning cereal. Throw caution to the wind and enjoy this ice cream for breakfast or any time of day. Add a small splash of bourbon if you need help recovering from last night's bad decisions.

3 cups (710ml) whole milk

1 ¾ cups (414ml) heavy cream, divided

⅛ tsp salt

2 cups (56g) cornflakes

½ tsp ground cinnamon

3 medium-size ripe bananas, sliced into ½" (1.3cm) pieces

⅓ cup (70g) packed light brown sugar

1 tbsp (14g) unsalted butter, cut into small pieces

½ tsp vanilla extract

1 tsp freshly squeezed lemon juice

Combine the milk, ¼ cup (59ml) of the cream and salt in a medium saucepan. Place over medium heat and bring to a low boil. Remove from the heat, add the cornflakes and cinnamon, cover and steep at room temperature for 1 hour.

Meanwhile, preheat the oven to 400°F (200°C, or gas mark 6). Toss the bananas with the brown sugar and butter in a small (2-quart [1.8L]) baking dish. Bake for 40 minutes, stirring once during baking, until the bananas are browned and cooked through. Scrape the contents of the dish (bananas and sugar syrup) into a blender; set aside.

When the milk mixture is finished steeping, pour it through a sieve into a medium bowl. Press cornflakes with the back of a wooden spoon to remove as much moisture as possible. Discard the mushy cornflakes. *The cereal soaks up a lot of moisture; yield of cornflake-infused milk should be about 1 ½ cups (355 ml).* Combine the banana mixture, cornflake-infused milk, remaining 1 ½ cups (355ml) cream, vanilla, and lemon juice in the blender and purée until smooth. Cover and chill overnight.

Pour the ice cream base into an ice cream maker and churn according to the manufacturer's instructions. Transfer to a freezer-safe container and freeze until firm, at least 4 hours.

Note: Prefer another cereal for breakfast? Substitute your favorite cereal for the cornflakes and make this ice cream your Breakfast of Champions.

King Cake Ice Cream

MAKES 1 QUART (940ML)

A much-loved tradition of the carnival season in New Orleans is the baking and eating of king cake. Gooey, spicy cinnamon is twisted into a circle of soft, airy pastry bread and topped with sugar or icing. The result is a mouthwatering dessert reminiscent of a cinnamon roll but monstrously better. Many bakeries add fillings to their cake, and my favorite filling is cream cheese. Inspired by my love of king cake, this flavor is a decadent combination of cinnamon and cream cheese. Enjoy the carnival season year-round with this ice cream.

CINNAMON SWIRL

½ cup (110g) packed brown sugar

⅓ cup (79ml) water

2 tbsp (29g) unsalted butter

1 tsp (3g) cornstarch

½ tsp ground cinnamon

ICE CREAM BASE

1 cup (237ml) whole milk, divided

1 ½ cups (355ml) heavy cream, divided

¾ cup (150g) sugar

Five 3" (7.5cm) cinnamon sticks

1 tbsp (9g) cornstarch

8 oz (224g) cream cheese, softened

⅛ tsp salt

½ tsp vanilla extract

To prepare the cinnamon swirl, combine the brown sugar, water, butter, cornstarch and cinnamon in a small saucepan. Place over medium heat and stir until the butter melts and all the ingredients are combined, 2 minutes. Continue stirring until the mixture thickens and reaches the consistency of maple syrup, 5 minutes. Remove from the heat and cool completely before adding to the ice cream.

To make the ice cream base, reserve 2 tablespoons (30ml) of the milk. Combine 1 cup (237ml) of the cream, remaining milk, sugar and cinnamon sticks in a medium saucepan and place over medium-high heat. Once the mixture is hot and steam begins to rise, remove from the heat, cover and let steep at room temperature for 1 hour.

When steeping is almost complete, whisk the reserved 2 tablespoons (30ml) milk and the cornstarch in a small bowl and set aside. Whisk the cream cheese and salt in a medium bowl; set aside. Fill a large bowl with ice water.

When steeping is complete, remove the cinnamon sticks from the milk mixture with a slotted spoon. Add the remaining ½ cup (118ml) cream to the cinnamon-infused milk and begin rewarming. Bring the milk mixture to a low boil and cook over medium heat for 3 minutes. Remove the milk mixture from the heat and gradually whisk in the cornstarch mixture. Return to a boil and cook over moderately high heat until the mixture is slightly thickened, about 1 minute. Pour into bowl with cream cheese, whisk thouroughly. Set the bowl in the ice water bath to cool, 20 minutes, whisking occasionally. Add the vanilla. Cover and refrigerate until well chilled, at least 4 hours or overnight.

When ready to churn, whisk the ice cream base and pour into an ice cream maker. Churn according to the manufacturer's instructions. Spoon a small layer of cinnamon swirl into a freezer-safe container and lightly spoon a layer of ice cream on top. Continue to alternate layers of cinnamon swirl and ice cream until the container is full, gently swirling with a spoon (careful not to muddy the ice cream). Freeze until firm, at least 4 hours.

Mint Julep Ice Cream

MAKES 1 QUART (940ML)

Besides being an ingredient in bourbon ball candies (page 45), bourbon makes some spectacular drinks. Mint juleps, with muddled mint, fine sugar and bourbon, are the drink of choice at Kentucky's famous Derby parties and parties throughout the South. For those who enjoy dessert as much as a cocktail, this ice cream is a perfect treat for party goers or for slow savoring on a hot summer day.

1 ½ cups (355ml) whole milk, divided

1 tbsp (9g) cornstarch

1 ¾ cups (414ml) heavy cream

⅔ cup (133g) sugar

⅓ cup (32g) loosely packed mint leaves

⅛ tsp salt

2 tbsp (30 ml) bourbon

Fill a large bowl with ice water. In a small bowl, combine 2 tablespoons (30ml) of the milk with the cornstarch, whisk and set aside. Combine the remaining milk, cream and sugar in a large saucepan. Warm over medium heat until the mixture is hot and begins to bubble. Remove from the heat, add the mint and steep at room temperature for 20 minutes. Pour the mint-infused milk through a fine-mesh sieve, pressing on the back of the mint with a wooden spoon to extract as much flavor as possible.

Return the mint-infused milk to a medium saucepan and bring to a low boil over medium heat. Remove from the heat and gradually whisk in the cornstarch mixture. Return to a boil and cook over moderately high heat until the mixture is slightly thickened, about 1 minute. Remove from the heat and pour into a medium bowl. Whisk in the salt. Set the bowl in the ice water bath to cool, 20 minutes, whisking occasionally. Cover and chill overnight.

Once chilled, add the bourbon and stir to combine. Pour the ice cream base into an ice cream maker and churn according to the manufacturer's instructions. Transfer to a freezer-safe container and freeze overnight.

Red Velvet Ice Cream

MAKES 1 GENEROUS QUART (940ML)

Baked desserts are often great inspiration for ice cream flavors. One delicious inspiration for ice cream is red velvet cake. My favorite part of red velvet cake is the cream cheese icing, so this scoop is a "reversed" version of red velvet cake with pieces of cake mixed into a cream cheese ice cream base, creating the perfect frozen alternative to a classic Southern cake.

3 red velvet cupcakes, frosting removed

12 oz (340g) cream cheese

1 ½ cups (355ml) sour cream

1 cup (200g) sugar

½ cup (118ml) heavy cream

½ cup (118ml) buttermilk

¼ tsp vanilla extract

Pinch of salt

Prepare your favorite red velvet cupcake recipe or buy your favorite prepared cupcakes. If you choose to bake cupcakes, allow the cupcakes to cool completely before adding to the ice cream.

Cut the cream cheese into small pieces and place in a blender or food processor. Add the sour cream, sugar, cream, buttermilk, vanilla and salt and blend until smooth. Cover and refrigerate until well chilled, at least 2 hours.

Once chilled, pour the ice cream base into an ice cream maker and churn according to the manufacturer's instructions. Chop the cupcakes into ½-inch (1.3cm) cubes. When churning is complete, gently fold in the cupcake pieces. Transfer to a freezer-safe container and top with a few pieces of cupcake. Freeze until firm, at least 4 hours.

Blueberry Mojito Ice Cream

MAKES 3 CUPS (705ML)

Fruity, full of citrus, with a hint of mint and a smack of rum, this ice cream tastes exactly like the real thing. If you have visited New Orleans, you may have stopped by St. Joe's Bar, the inspiration for this ice cream. At St. Joe's they muddle fresh blueberries and mint into a mix of sugar and alcohol for a truly refreshing drink. After a hot summer day of picking blueberries, I was inspired to make this cool drink into an equally refreshing scoop.

LIME SYRUP

¼ cup (59ml) lime juice

¼ cup (50g) sugar

ICE CREAM BASE

1 cup (230g) fresh or frozen blueberries

½ cup (100g) sugar

1 cup (237ml) whole milk, divided

1 tbsp (9g) cornstarch

1 ¼ cups (295ml) heavy cream

¼ cup (24g) packed mint leaves

1 ½ tbsp (22ml) white rum

To make the lime syrup, combine the juice and ¼ cup (50g) sugar in a small saucepan and place over medium heat. Heat until the sugar is dissolved, 1 to 2 minutes. Pour into a small bowl, cover and refrigerate until completely cool.

To make the ice cream base, combine the blueberries and ½ cup (100g) sugar in a small saucepan. Warm over medium heat, stirring frequently, until the mixture is simmering and slightly reduced and the berries release their juices. Remove from the heat and set aside.

Fill a large bowl with ice water. In a small bowl, combine 2 tablespoons (30ml) of the milk with the cornstarch, whisk and set aside. Combine the remaining milk and cream in a medium saucepan and place over medium heat. When the mixture is hot and begins to bubble, remove from the heat, add the mint and steep at room temperature for 20 minutes. Pour the mint-infused milk through a fine-mesh sieve, pressing on the back of the mint with a wooden spoon to extract as much flavor as possible.

Return the mint-infused milk to a medium saucepan and bring to a low boil over medium heat. Remove from the heat and gradually whisk in the cornstarch mixture. Return to a boil and cook over moderately high heat until the mixture is slightly thickened, about 30 seconds. Remove from the heat and pour into a medium bowl. Set the bowl in the ice water bath to cool, 20 minutes, whisking occasionally. Combine the blueberry mixture and cooled ice cream base in a blender and blend until the berries are fully incorporated. Cover and refrigerate until well chilled, at least 4 hours or overnight.

Whisk the chilled ice cream base, and add the lime syrup and rum. Pour the ice cream base into an ice cream maker and churn according to the manufacturer's instructions. Transfer to a freezer-safe container and freeze until firm, at least 4 hours.

Toasted Marshmallow Ice Cream

MAKES 1 QUART (940ML)

S'mores are one of the best American creations. Roasting marshmallows over an open fire, pulling the gooey marshmallow off the stick you found in the woods, and watching it ooze all over as you squeeze it between two graham crackers and a piece of chocolate is a piece of heaven. The dark caramelized sugar on a toasted marshmallow is a flavor all its own. Scoop this ice cream at your next backyard get-together and you will be everyone's favorite.

7 oz (200g) mini marshmallows

1 ½ cups (355ml) whole milk

1 ¾ cups (414ml) heavy cream

⅓ cup (67g) sugar

⅛ teaspoon salt

½ tsp vanilla extract

Preheat the oven to 350°F (180°C, or gas mark 4). Line a rimmed baking sheet with parchment, allowing the parchment to hang over the edges of the pan. Spread out the mini marshmallows on the baking sheet. Bake until dark brown in color, with some marshmallows beginning to burn, 12 to 14 minutes. Remove from the oven and set aside.

Fill a large bowl with ice water and set aside. Combine the milk, heavy cream and sugar in a medium saucepan and place over medium heat. Bring the milk mixture to a low boil. Cook until the sugar dissolves, 3 minutes. Reduce the heat to low and add the toasted marshmallows. Whisk until the marshmallows melt, 5 minutes. Pour into a medium bowl. Whisk in the salt. Set the bowl in the ice water bath to cool, 20 minutes, whisking occasionally. Add the vanilla. Cover and chill overnight.

Once chilled, pour the ice cream base into an ice cream maker and churn according to the manufacturer's instructions. Pack the ice cream into a freezer-safe container. Freeze until firm, at least 4 hours.

Serving suggestion: Top with a scoop of Cow Patty Ice Cream (page 84) or other chocolate ice cream, sprinkle with graham cracker crumbs and you have a cool s'more in a bowl.

Chocolate Porter Ice Cream

MAKES 1 QUART (940ML)

A recent trip to Colorado opened my eyes to the beautiful mountains of the Rockies as well as the plethora of microbrews in the state. If you are a beer lover, then you must make a pilgrimage to Colorado. Beer, with its complexity and variety of flavor, is an excellent ingredient in ice cream. Chocolate Porter Ice Cream is a grown-up version of a classic dark chocolate scoop. Toasty and hoppy porter lends a slight bitterness to the ice cream that complements and highlights the dark chocolate flavor. Add a scoop to a pint of beer for a delicious ice cream float.

CHOCOLATE LIQUOR

½ cup (56g) cocoa powder

⅓ cup (79ml) water

⅓ cup (67g) sugar

2 oz (56g) bittersweet chocolate, chopped

¼ tsp salt

ICE CREAM BASE

¾ cup (177ml) whole milk, divided

1 tbsp cornstarch

1 ½ cups (355ml) heavy cream

1 cup (237ml) evaporated milk

⅓ cup (67g) sugar

¼ tsp vanilla extract

¾ cup (177ml) porter beer

To make the chocolate liquor, combine the cocoa powder, water and sugar in a small saucepan. Place the saucepan over medium-low heat and bring to a low boil, whisking constantly. As soon as you see bubbles, remove from the heat and add the bittersweet chocolate. Let sit for 2 minutes and then stir the chocolate liquor until smooth. Whisk the chocolate liquor and salt in a medium bowl and set aside.

To make the ice cream base, fill a large bowl with ice water and set aside. In a small bowl, whisk 2 tablespoons (30ml) of the milk and cornstarch; set aside. Combine the remaining milk, cream, evaporated milk and sugar in a medium saucepan and place over medium heat. Bring the milk mixture to a low boil. Cook until the sugar dissolves, 3 minutes.

Remove the milk mixture from the heat and gradually whisk in the cornstarch mixture. Return to a boil and cook over moderately high heat until the mixture is slightly thickened, about 1 minute. Pour into a medium bowl. Set the bowl in the ice water bath to cool, 20 minutes, whisking occasionally. Cover and refrigerate until well chilled, at least 4 hours or overnight.

When ready to churn, add the vanilla and beer. Pour the ice cream base into an ice cream machine and churn according to the manufacturer's instructions. Transfer to a freezer-safe container and freeze until firm, at least 4 hours.

Ginger Chocolate Chunk Ice Cream

MAKES 1 QUART (940ML)

Ginger is spicy and seductive. Once it is familiar to you, the flavor is distinctive and adds a layer of complexity to many dishes. This flavorful root has many uses ranging from an ingredient in medicine to savory spices to flavoring drinks. Ginger is an excellent ingredient for ice cream because it adds both spice and heat, resulting in a contrast of hot and cold and an explosion of flavor in every bite. It is a perfect complement to any sweet or spicy dessert.

5 oz (85g) fresh ginger

1 ½ cups (355ml) whole milk, divided

1 ¾ cups (414ml) heavy cream, divided

⅔ cup (133g) sugar

1 tbsp (9g) cornstarch

⅛ tsp salt

1 cup (250g) chopped chocolate-covered ginger*

Cut the fresh ginger into thin slices. Transfer to a medium saucepan and cover with ½ inch (1.3cm) of water. Place over high heat and bring to a boil. Boil for 2 minutes, remove from the heat and pour through a fine-mesh sieve. Discard the liquid. Return the ginger slices to the saucepan and add 1 ¼ cups (295ml) of the milk, ¾ cup (177ml) of the cream and the sugar. Warm the mixture over medium heat until hot and bubbles begin to form, 3 to 4 minutes. Turn off the heat, cover and steep for 1 hour.

Fill a large bowl with ice water and set aside. In a small bowl, combine remaining the ¼ cup (59ml) milk with the cornstarch, whisk and set aside. Pour the ginger-infused milk through a fine-mesh sieve to remove the ginger slices. Return the infused milk to the medium saucepan and add the remaining 1 cup (237ml) cream. Place over medium heat and bring to a low boil. Cook for 3 minutes.

Remove the milk mixture from the heat and gradually whisk in the cornstarch mixture. Return to a boil and cook over moderately high heat until the mixture is slightly thickened, about 1 minute. Remove from the heat and pour into a medium bowl. Whisk in the salt. Set the bowl in the ice water bath to cool, 20 minutes, whisking occasionally. Cover and refrigerate until well chilled, at least 4 hours or overnight.

Once chilled, pour the ice cream base into an ice cream maker and churn according to the manufacturer's instructions. When churning is complete, gently fold in the chocolate-covered ginger pieces. Transfer to a freezer-safe container and freeze until firm, at least 4 hours.

If you cannot find chocolate-covered ginger, you may substitute ½ cup (87g) chocolate chips plus ½ cup (50g) chopped crystalized ginger for an equally spicy and sweet treat.

Prickly Pear Coconut Ice Cream

MAKES 3 CUPS (705ML)

Many of my ice cream flavors are inspired by experiences and memories. One such inspirational experience was a trip to the Grand Canyon and Sedona, Arizona. This region of the United States possesses a special spirit, a spirit that makes you feel humbled and free at the same time, and I fell in love with it. A famous food from the region is the prickly pear, a bright pink fruit that grows on a cactus. The flavor is both tart and sweet, often described as tasting like a tart watermelon, and it lends itself well to fruity cocktails and sweet treats. The sweet and creamy coconut and tart prickly pear in this ice cream are winning combination.

1 ¾ cups (414ml) regular coconut milk

¾ cup (177ml) prickly pear syrup

1 to 2 tbsp (15 to 30ml) fresh lime juice

Pinch of salt

Pour coconut milk into a medium bowl. Whisk until smooth. Add the prickly pear syrup, lime juice and salt. Whisk until combined. Chill in the refrigerator until completely cold, about 2 hours. Once chilled, pour into an ice cream maker and churn according to the manufacturer's instructions. Transfer to a freezer-safe container and freeze until firm, about 4 hours.

Tip: Prickly pear syrup can be found at most specialty stores in the Southwest or ordered online. If you are lucky enough to have access to real prickly pear fruit, there are several recipes online that describe how to make your own prickly pear syrup.

Rosemary Honey Walnut Ice Cream

MAKES 1 QUART (940ML)

One day during my ice cream adventures, I came upon an ice cream flavored with balsam fir extract. It was probably one of the most interesting flavors I have ever tasted, but I could not get past the woodsy essence of the ice cream. It was delicious after one spoonful, but hard to eat after a few more. I set out to make a similar, herby tasting ice cream but one that was a little more tolerable to my palate. Rosemary was the perfect alternative, with a distinctive sweet pine taste that is complemented by golden honey and toasted, buttery almonds. I could eat a whole bowl of this flavor.

¾ cup (87g) raw walnuts

1 ½ cups (355ml) whole milk, divided

1 tbsp (9g) cornstarch

1 ¾ cups (414ml) heavy cream

⅓ cup (67g) sugar

⅓ cup (79ml) mild honey

1 tsp minced rosemary

¼ tsp salt

Preheat the oven to 350°F (180°C, or gas mark 4). Spread the walnuts on a parchment- or silicone-lined rimmed baking sheet. Bake for 10 minutes, or until the walnuts are toasted and fragrant, stirring every 5 minutes. Check the walnuts every few minutes to prevent burning. Cool to room temperature and chop. Store in a covered container until ready to use.

Fill a large bowl with ice water. In a small bowl, combine 2 tablespoons (30ml) of the milk with the cornstarch, whisk and set aside. Combine the remaining milk with the heavy cream, sugar and honey in a medium saucepan and place over medium heat. Bring the milk mixture to a low boil. Cook until the sugar and honey dissolve, 3 minutes.

Remove the milk mixture from the heat and gradually whisk in the cornstarch mixture. Return to a boil and cook over moderately high heat until the mixture is slightly thickened, about 1 minute. Pour into a medium bowl. Whisk in the rosemary and salt. Set the bowl in the ice water bath to cool, 20 minutes, whisking occasionally. Cover and refrigerate until well chilled, at least 4 hours or overnight.

Once chilled, pour the ice cream base through a fine-mesh sieve to remove the rosemary pieces. Pour into an ice cream maker and churn according to the manufacturer's instructions. When churning is complete, gently fold in the walnut pieces. Transfer to a freezer-safe container and freeze until firm, at least 4 hours.

Wham Bam, Thank You Graham Ice Cream

MAKES 1 QUART (940ML)

Graham crackers are good for more than eating straight from the box. Add butter and they make a wonderful crust or add to chocolate and marshmallows for a campfire treat. Despite their many uses, my favorite way to eat graham crackers is with a glass of milk. When graham crackers are steeped in milk and cream and churned into a scoop, it is an even better version of my favorite snack. Serve with a scoop of a Key Lime Pie Ice Cream (page 83) for a heavenly treat.

1 ½ cups (355ml) whole milk, divided

1 tbsp (9g) cornstarch

1 ¾ cups (414ml) heavy cream

⅔ cup (133g) sugar

⅛ tsp salt

¾ cup (67g) chopped graham crackers

½ cup (45g) crumbled graham crackers (optional)

Fill a large bowl with ice water. In a small bowl, combine 2 tablespoons (30ml) of the milk with the cornstarch, whisk and set aside. Combine the remaining milk with the heavy cream and sugar in a medium saucepan and place over medium heat. Bring the milk mixture to a low boil. Cook until the sugar dissolves, 3 minutes.

Remove the milk mixture from the heat and gradually whisk in the cornstarch mixture. Return to a boil and cook over moderately high heat until the mixture is slightly thickened, about 1 minute. Pour into a medium bowl. Whisk in the salt. Add the ¾ cup (67g) chopped graham crackers to the hot milk mixture. Steep for 30 minutes to dissolve the crackers and impart flavor. Whisk to incorporate the crackers. Set the bowl in the ice water bath to cool, 20 minutes, whisking occasionally. Cover and refrigerate overnight.

Once chilled, whisk the ice cream base to break up any remaining cookie pieces. Pour into an ice cream maker and churn according to the manufacturer's instructions. Transfer to a freezer-safe container and freeze until firm, at least 4 hours.

Tip: Feel free to play around with this recipe. Add 2 tablespoons (30ml) honey to the cooking process for a honey graham flavor. Add ½ teaspoon ground cinnamon to the cooking process for a cinnamon graham flavor.

Sandy Beach Ice Cream

MAKES 1 QUART (940ML)

A trip to the beach awakens my senses with the smell of coconut suntan lotion, the crunch of the sand between my toes and the warm sun on my face. This scoop of smooth, toasted coconut ice cream layered with crunchy, sandy pieces of shortbread cookie is what I call the beach in a scoop.

1 ½ cups (105g) unsweetened shredded coconut

1 ½ cups (355ml) whole milk, divided

1 ¾ cups (414ml) heavy cream

¾ cup (150g) sugar

1 vanilla bean

1 tbsp (9g) cornstarch

⅛ tsp salt

1 cup (250g) chopped shortbread cookies, frozen

Preheat the oven to 350°F (180°C, or gas mark 4). Spread the coconut in an even layer on a baking sheet and bake for 8 minutes, or until the coconut is fragrant and golden brown. Toss the coconut frequently to ensure even toasting. Reserve ¼ cup (17g) of the toasted coconut to top the ice cream.

In a medium saucepan, combine ¾ cup (177ml) of the milk, heavy cream, sugar and remaining 1¼ cups (88g) toasted coconut. Cut open the vanilla bean and scrape all the vanilla seeds into the milk mixture, adding the pod as well. Warm over medium heat until the mixture is hot and steam begins to rise, 3 to 4 minutes. Cover, remove from the heat and let steep at room temperature for 1 hour.

When steeping is almost complete, fill a large bowl with ice water. In a small bowl, combine 2 tablespoons (30ml) of the milk with the cornstarch, whisk and set aside. Strain the coconut-infused liquid through a sieve into another medium saucepan. Press down firmly on the coconut to extract as much of the flavor as possible. Discard the coconut and vanilla bean pod.

Add the remaining milk to the coconut-infused mixture and return the mixture to medium heat. Bring to a low boil and boil for 3 minutes. Remove the milk mixture from the heat and gradually whisk in the cornstarch mixture. Return to a boil and cook over moderately high heat until the mixture is slightly thickened, about 1 minute. Pour into a medium bowl and whisk in the salt. Set the bowl in the ice water bath to cool, 20 minutes, whisking occasionally. Cover and refrigerate until well chilled, at least 4 hours or overnight.

Once chilled, pour the ice cream base into an ice cream maker and churn according to the manufacturer's instructions. When the ice cream is finished churning, gently fold in the shortbread pieces. Transfer to a freezer-safe container and freeze until firm, at least 4 hours. When serving, sprinkle with the reserved toasted coconut.

Peppermint Fleck Ice Cream

MAKES 1 QUART (940ML)

Every year I try to grow a garden. Unfortunately, I did not inherit my mother's green thumb. Some years I am lucky and other years not so much. Growing herbs, however, is a no-brainer. As long as they stay watered, herbs will grow for me. I love growing a variety of herbs, from the basic basil, thyme and oregano to the more exotic lemongrass and pineapple sage. I also like to grow a variety of mints. It is practically a weed and hard to kill, so it is perfect for me. When fresh mint is steeped in sweet cream and flecked with pieces of dark chocolate, I quickly forget about my garden troubles.

- 1 ½ cups (355ml) whole milk, divided
- 1 tbsp (9g) cornstarch
- 1 ¾ cups (414ml) heavy cream
- ⅔ cup (133g) sugar
- ⅛ tsp salt
- 1 cup (96g) peppermint leaves
- 3 oz (84g) dark chocolate, chopped

Fill a large bowl with ice water. In a small bowl, combine 2 tablespoons (30ml) of the milk with the cornstarch, whisk and set aside. Combine the remaining milk with the heavy cream and sugar in a medium saucepan and place over medium heat. Bring the milk mixture to a low boil. Cook until the sugar dissolves, 3 minutes. Remove the milk mixture from the heat and gradually whisk in the cornstarch mixture. Return to a boil and cook over moderately high heat until the mixture is slightly thickened, about 1 minute. Pour into a medium bowl. Whisk in the salt. Add the peppermint leaves and steep at room temperature for 20 minutes.

Pour the peppermint-infused milk through a fine-mesh sieve into a medium bowl, pressing on the back of the mint with a wooden spoon to extract as much flavor as possible. Discard the mint. Set the bowl in the ice water bath to cool, 20 minutes, whisking occasionally. Cover and refrigerate until well chilled, at least 4 hours or overnight.

Once chilled, pour the ice cream base into an ice cream maker and churn according to the manufacturer's instructions. When churning is near completion, use a double boiler to melt the dark chocolate until completely smooth. Transfer the melted chocolate to a small zip-top bag and keep warm.

When the ice cream is finished and begins to pull away from the sides of the canister, cut a small hole in the corner of the chocolate bag and slowly drizzle a small stream of warm chocolate into the churning ice cream. *If the ice cream isn't moving well, the chocolate may be getting caught on the dasher, so move the ice cream away from the dasher using a spoon.* (If you have trouble with the drizzle method, you can also alternate layers of drizzled chocolate with finished ice cream as you scoop it into a container; do not stir.) Complete churning and transfer to a freezer-safe container. Freeze until firm, at least 4 hours.

Note: Looking for a more subtle peppermint flavor? Reduce the amount of peppermint leaves to ¾ cup (72g) or experiment to find your ideal amount of peppermint.

Goat Cheese Ice Cream with Pickled Blueberries

MAKES 1 QUART (940ML)

Goat cheese and I did not always get along, but eventually, I overcame my fear and began to love the rich and tangy quality. The addition of cheese makes this scoop extra creamy, and the tangy notes pair beautifully with the sweet and spicy blueberries.

- -

PICKLED BLUEBERRIES

3 cloves

3 allspice berries

¼ tsp fennel seeds

¼ tsp whole black peppercorns

1 cinnamon stick

6 tablespoons (90ml) champagne or white wine vinegar

1 pint (340g) fresh blueberries

½ cup (100g) sugar

ICE CREAM BASE

4 oz (112g) fresh goat cheese, softened

¼ tsp salt

1 ½ cups (355ml) whole milk, divided

1 tbsp (9g) cornstarch

1 ¾ cups (414ml) heavy cream

⅔ cup (133g) sugar

Preparing the pickled blueberries is a two-day process. Begin by combining the spices in a small piece of cheesecloth and tying with twine. Combine the spice bag and vinegar in a large saucepan and bring to a simmer over medium heat. Cover and let simmer for 5 minutes. Uncover and add the blueberries, heating until the berries begin to swell and darken (do not allow the berries to burst), about 8 minutes. Remove from the heat, cover and let stand at room temperature for 12 hours.

Place a colander over a large bowl. Remove the spice bag from the saucepan and gently pour the blueberry mixture through a colander, catching all of the liquid in the bowl. Pour the blueberries into a medium container. Return the liquid to the saucepan, add the sugar and bring to a boil. Boil for 5 minutes, or until the liquid begins to thicken into a syrup. Add the syrup to the blueberries. Chill completely before using in the ice cream.

To make the ice cream base, fill a large bowl with ice water. Whisk the goat cheese and salt in a medium bowl until smooth. In a small bowl, combine 2 tablespoons (30ml) of the milk with the cornstarch, whisk and set aside. Combine the remaining milk with the heavy cream and sugar in a medium saucepan and place over medium heat. Bring the milk mixture to a low boil. Cook until the sugar dissolves, 3 minutes.

Remove the milk mixture from the heat and gradually whisk in the cornstarch mixture. Return to a boil and cook over moderately high heat until the mixture is slightly thickened, about 1 minute. Pour the milk mixture into the goat cheese mixture and whisk until smooth. Set the bowl in the ice water bath to cool, 20 minutes, whisking occasionally. Cover and refrigerate until well chilled, at least 4 hours or overnight.

Once chilled, pour the ice cream base into an ice cream maker and churn according to the manufacturer's instructions. Spoon a small layer of pickled blueberries into a freezer-safe container and lightly spoon a layer of ice cream on top. Continue to alternate layers of pickled blueberries and ice cream until the container is full. Freeze until firm, at least 4 hours.

Mai Tai Ice Cream

MAKES 1 QUART (940ML)

The mai tai cocktail became popular in the midcentury, and it is frequently served at tiki-themed restaurants, such as the self-proclaimed creator Trader Vic's in Oakland, California. Regardless of where the drink is served, the mai tai is a delicious cocktail with an explosion of flavor. It is traditionally made with rum, curaçao and lime, but fruit juices have been added over the years to create a sweeter drink. Inspired by the sweeter tropical version, this is an ice cream that will make you want to party!

3 egg yolks

1 ¼ cups (295ml) heavy cream, divided

1 cup (200g) sugar

½ cup (118ml) pineapple juice

½ cup (118ml) peach or passion fruit nectar

½ cup (118ml) guava nectar

1 tbsp (15ml) fresh lime juice

2 tsp grenadine

2 tsp dark rum

Whisk the egg yolks in a medium bowl. Combine ¾ cup (177ml) of the heavy cream and the sugar in a medium saucepan and warm over medium heat until the sugar dissolves, 3 minutes. Temper the eggs by slowly pouring ½ cup (118ml) of the warmed cream mixture into the yolks, whisking constantly until combined. Return the warmed yolks to the pan with the remaining cream mixture. Heat the custard over medium-low heat, stirring constantly, until the custard thickens and coats the back of a spoon.

Remove the custard from the heat and pour through a fine-mesh sieve into a medium bowl. Add the remaining ½ cup (118ml) heavy cream. Stir well and cool to room temperature. Once cool, add the fruit juices and grenadine. Mix thoroughly, cover and refrigerate until well chilled, at least 4 hours or overnight.

When the ice cream base is chilled, add the rum and pour into an ice cream maker. Churn according to the manufacturer's instructions. Transfer to a freezer-safe container and freeze for at least 4 hours. Serve with an additional splash of dark rum for a more pronounced cocktail flavor.

Spiced Strawberry Rhubarb Swirl Ice Cream

MAKES 1 QUART (940ML)

Berry season is possibly one of my favorite times of year. It is a season that inspires homemade pies, jams and, of course, ice cream. Rhubarb and strawberries both arrive in early spring and they are perfect recipe companions. This spicy and tart scoop is the result of leftover ground spices in the kitchen plus a discussion of ice cream over jam and toast. Cinnamon, cardamom and star anise come alive with a swirl of sweet strawberry rhubarb. It is a refreshing scoop to enjoy in early spring or any time of year.

STRAWBERRY RHUBARB SWIRL

1 cup (226g) chopped rhubarb

1 cup (200g) mashed strawberries

½ cup (100g) sugar

½ tsp vanilla extract

ICE CREAM BASE

1 ½ cups (355ml) whole milk, divided

1 tbsp (9g) cornstarch

1 ¾ cups (414ml) heavy cream

⅔ cup (133g) sugar

¼ tsp ground star anise

¼ tsp ground cardamom

¼ tsp ground cinnamon

⅛ tsp salt

To make the strawberry rhubarb swirl, combine the rhubarb, strawberries and sugar in a medium saucepan. Stir until the berries have begun to macerate, then place over medium-low heat. Cook, stirring occasionally, until the rhubarb and strawberries are broken down, 10 to 15 minutes. Reduce the heat to low and simmer until the mixture is reduced by half of its original volume, about 10 minutes. Remove from the heat and cool to room temperature. Stir in the vanilla. Cover and chill completely before swirling in the ice cream.

To make the ice cream base, fill a large bowl with ice water. In a small bowl, combine 2 tablespoons (30ml) of the milk with the cornstarch, whisk and set aside. Combine the remaining milk with the heavy cream, sugar, star anise, cardamom and cinnamon in a medium saucepan. Place over medium heat and bring the milk mixture to a low boil. Cook until the sugar dissolves, 3 minutes.

Remove the milk mixture from the heat and gradually whisk in the cornstarch mixture. Return to a boil and cook over moderately high heat until the mixture is slightly thickened, about 1 minute. Pour into a medium bowl and whisk in the salt. Set the bowl in the ice water bath to cool, 20 minutes, whisking occasionally. Cover and refrigerate until well chilled, at least 4 hours or overnight.

Once chilled, pour the ice cream base into an ice cream maker and churn according to the manufacturer's instructions. Spoon a small layer of strawberry rhubarb swirl into a freezer-safe container and lightly spoon a layer of ice cream on top. Continue to alternate layers of fruit swirl and ice cream until the container is full, gently swirling with a spoon (careful not to muddy the ice cream). Freeze until firm, at least 4 hours.

Chocolate Coconut Macadamia Nut Ice Cream

MAKES 1 QUART (940ML)

Macadamia nuts are a well-loved and ubiquitous ingredient in Hawaii. Grown on the islands, these beloved nuts are used in both savory and sweet dishes. During a recent trip to Hawaii, I discovered the winning combination of chocolate, coconut and macadamia nuts, and from that moment I knew that I needed to create an ice cream based on the flavors. Enjoy this decadent and crunchy scoop and you may just take a trip to the islands.

CHOCOLATE LIQUOR

⅓ cup (37g) cocoa powder

⅓ cup (79ml) water

⅓ cup (67g) sugar

2 oz (56g) bittersweet chocolate, chopped

¼ tsp salt

ICE CREAM BASE

½ cup (118ml) whole milk, divided

1 tbsp (9g) cornstarch

1 ½ cups (355ml) heavy cream

1 ¼ cups (295ml) coconut milk

⅓ cup (67g) sugar

¼ tsp vanilla extract

½ cup (38g) unsweetened shredded coconut

¾ cup (100g) chopped macadamia nuts

To make the chocolate liquor, combine the cocoa powder, water and sugar in a small saucepan. Place the saucepan over medium-low heat and bring to a low boil, whisking frequently. As soon as the mixture begins to boil, remove from the heat and add the bittersweet chocolate. Let sit for 2 minutes, and then stir the chocolate liquor until smooth. Whisk the chocolate liquor and pour into a medium bowl. Add the salt, whisk and set aside.

To make the ice cream base, fill a large bowl with ice water and set aside. In a small bowl, combine 2 tablespoons (30ml) of the whole milk with the cornstarch, whisk and set aside. Combine the remaining whole milk, cream, coconut milk and sugar in a medium saucepan. Place over medium heat and bring the milk mixture to a low boil. Cook until the sugar dissolves, 2 to 3 minutes.

Remove the milk mixture from the heat and gradually whisk in the cornstarch mixture. Return to a boil and cook over moderately high heat until the mixture is slightly thickened, about 1 minute. Pour through a fine-mesh sieve into the bowl with the chocolate liquor. Set the bowl in the ice water bath to cool, 20 minutes, whisking occasionally. Add the vanilla and whisk to combine. Cover and refrigerate until well chilled, at least 4 hours or overnight.

Pour the ice cream base into an ice cream machine and churn according to the manufacturer's instructions. When churning is complete, gently fold in the coconut and macadamia nuts. Transfer to a freezer-safe container and freeze until firm, at least 4 hours. The longer the ice cream rests in the freezer, the more coconut flavor will be imparted into the ice cream by the shredded coconut.

Juniper Gin Ice Cream

MAKES 1 QUART (940ML)

Gin o'clock, anyone? Second only to beer, gin is one of my favorite forms of alcohol. After several gin and tonics one evening, I decided that I must make a scoop inspired by my favorite cocktail. I did a little research on my preferred liquor and discovered that in order for a liquor to be called gin, it must be flavored predominantly with juniper. London Dry Gin is a classic and popular gin and it works well in this ice cream because it complements the added juniper flavor. Next time you are in the mood for a cocktail, think of a cocktail scoop.

1 ½ cups (355ml) whole milk, divided

1 tbsp (9g) cornstarch

3 tbsp juniper berries

1 ¾ cups (414ml) heavy cream, divided

⅔ cup (133g) sugar

⅛ teaspoon salt

2 tbsp (30ml) London Dry Gin

Mix 2 tablespoons (30ml) of the milk and the cornstarch in a small bowl; set aside. Coarsely grind the juniper berries. Combine the juniper berries, remaining milk, ½ cup (118ml) of the cream and sugar in a medium saucepan. Warm over medium heat. When the mixture is hot and steam begins rise, remove from the heat, cover and let steep at room temperature for 1 hour.

Meanwhile, fill a large bowl with ice water. When steeping is complete, strain the juniper-infused mixture through a fine-mesh sieve to remove the juniper berries. Return the juniper-infused mixture to the medium saucepan, add the remaining 1 ¼ cups (296ml) cream and return to medium heat. Bring the mixture to a low boil and cook for 3 minutes. Remove from the heat and gradually whisk in the cornstarch mixture. Return to a boil and cook over moderately high heat until the mixture is slightly thickened, about 1 minute. Pour into a medium bowl. Whisk in the salt. Set the bowl in the ice water bath to cool, 20 minutes, whisking occasionally. Cover and chill overnight.

Once chilled, add the gin and whisk to combine. Pour into an ice cream maker and churn according to the manufacturer's instructions. Transfer to a freezer-safe container and freeze until firm, at least 4 hours.

Note: If you do not have a grinder, the juniper berries can be ground using a mortar and pestle or by placing them in a heavy-duty bag and cracking them with a heavy object, like a rolling pin.

Serving suggestion: Add a squeeze of lime juice for a gin and tonic flavor or a squeeze of lemon for a refreshing treat, or scoop into a cup of strong coffee for an affogato reminiscent of Dutch coffee.

Avocado Lime Ice Cream

MAKES 1 QUART (940ML)

The first time I tried avocado I was already an adult. Perhaps my lack of exposure to avocados was due to a limited culinary palate as a child, or because I did not live in California, or maybe I just thought they looked weird. No matter, because when I did try an avocado for the first time I was hooked. Smooth, creamy, nutty and healthy. Given its high fat content and natural creaminess, avocado is a perfect ice cream ingredient. The nutty flavor and creamy texture are evident in every bite and well balanced by the bright lime notes. Delicious and good for you!

LIME SYRUP

¼ cup (59ml) lime juice

¼ cup (50g) sugar

ICE CREAM BASE

3 medium ripe avocados

½ cup (100g) sugar

½ cup (118ml) plain yogurt

½ cup (118ml) milk

1 cup (237ml) heavy cream

Pinch of salt

To make the lime syrup, combine the lime juice and sugar in a small saucepan and place over medium heat. Heat until the sugar is dissolved, 2 to 3 minutes. Pour into a small bowl, cover and refrigerate until completely cool.

Before making the ice cream base, make sure that all ingredients are well chilled. Slice the avocados in half, remove the pits, and scoop out the flesh into a blender or food processor. Add the sugar, yogurt, milk, cream and salt. Blend until smooth. Add the lime syrup and pulse to combine (the mixture will be thick). Pour into an ice cream maker immediately* and churn according to the manufacturer's instructions. Transfer to a freezer-safe container and freeze until firm, at least 4 hours.

*Note: Immediate freezing is necessary to prevent browning. If you do not want to make the ice cream immediately, place the unchurned ice cream base directly into the freezer. When ready to use, thaw in the refrigerator and then follow the directions for churning.

Ube Ice Cream

MAKES 1 QUART (940ML)

Ube is a beauty of the vegetable world. With its bright violet-purple interior, this starchy and sweet staple is the perfect ingredient for sweet treats. Described as a frozen version of the popular Filipino dessert halayang, with a flavor similar to that of sweet red bean paste, this ice cream will satisfy any adventurous ice cream eater. Ube ice cream can be found in ice cream shops influenced by Filipino culture, such as Mitchell's in San Francisco, but now you can make it in your own home.

12 oz (340g) raw ube

1 ½ cups (355ml) whole milk, divided

1 tbsp (9g) cornstarch

1 ¾ cups (414ml) heavy cream

⅓ cup (67g) granulated sugar

⅓ cup (67g) packed dark brown sugar

⅛ tsp salt

1 tsp vanilla extract

Preheat the oven to 400°F (200°C, or gas mark 6). Wrap the ube in aluminum foil (do not remove the skin). Place on a baking sheet and bake for 30 to 40 minutes, until soft and a fork easily pierces the ube. Remove from the oven, unwrap and cool. Scrape the flesh out of the skin. Measure 1 ¼ cups (300g) ube, cover and refrigerate.

Fill a large bowl with ice water. In a small bowl, combine 2 tablespoons (30ml) of the milk with the cornstarch, whisk and set aside. Combine the remaining milk, cream, sugars and salt in a medium saucepan. Place the pan over medium-high heat, bring the mixture to a low boil and cook until the sugar dissolves, 3 minutes.

Remove the milk mixture from the heat and gradually whisk in the cornstarch mixture. Return to a boil and cook over medium-high heat until the mixture is slightly thickened, about 1 minute. Remove from the heat and pour into a medium bowl. Set the bowl in the ice water bath to cool, 20 minutes, whisking occasionally. Add the vanilla and whisk to combine. Cover and refrigerate until well chilled, at least 4 hours or overnight.

Combine 1 ½ cups (355 ml) of the chilled ice cream base and the roasted ube in a blender and purée until smooth. Pour into the bowl with the remaining ice cream base and whisk to combine. Pour the entire ice cream base into an ice cream maker and churn according to the manufacturer's instructions. Transfer to a freezer-safe container and freeze until firm, at least 4 hours.

Note: Ube is most likely found in Asian markets. If you cannot find raw ube in the produce section, check for frozen ube or purple yam. If you use frozen ube in this recipe, thaw and strain out as much water as possible before using.

Ingredients and Techniques

INGREDIENTS

The ingredients listed in each recipe are the best ingredients suggested by the author of the recipe. If you have trouble finding an ingredient, I would suggest looking online or visiting a specialty store. It is amazing what is available online these days, so even though it may take a little more time, your effort will pay off with the best-tasting ice cream. By all means, have fun experimenting with the recipes in this book or substitute ingredients, but just be aware that the flavor may not turn out exactly like the author intended. The best-quality ingredients make the best ice cream.

MILK AND CREAM
Seek out local dairy products for the freshest tasting ice creams. These milks and creams are typically minimally pasteurized and therefore will be more flavorful. If you are using non-homogenized dairy products, be sure to shake well before adding to the ice cream base. If shaking does not help homogenize the product, pour into a blender and blend until smooth, then add to the ice cream base.

EGGS
Source eggs locally for a fresher ingredient. Eggs laid by cage-free and pasture-raised chickens typically have deep golden yolks that will impart more flavor to your ice cream.

SUGAR
Cane sugar is my sugar of choice for ice cream because it is less processed and has a little molasses flavor, which adds to the depth of flavor in the ice cream.

STARCH
Several recipes in the cookbook call for tapioca starch or cornstarch, primarily recipes that do not use eggs. The purpose of this addition is to help capture some of the water and thicken the ice cream base, which improves the overall texture of the ice cream. Tapioca starch and cornstarch are interchangeable in these recipes.

COCOA AND CHOCOLATE
The majority of chocolate ice creams in the cookbook utilize a combination of cocoa powder and chocolate. If the type of cocoa powder is not specified in the recipe, then the choice is up to you. Dutch-processed cocoa powder is dark in color and typically imparts a more complex chocolate flavor. Non-alkalized cocoa powder is lighter in color and flavor, and it is often described as fruitier than its counterpart. When the recipe calls for chocolate, use the best-quality chocolate bar you can find. The darker the variety, the deeper the flavor you will add to your ice cream.

TECHNIQUES

WATER BATH

Many recipes instruct the reader to cool the ice cream base in a water bath. There are two major purposes for this step. For custard-based recipes, it is important to cool the base quickly to prevent the eggs from overcooking. In all of the recipes, it is also a good idea to cool the ice cream base before placing it in the refrigerator to prevent an unsafe increase in your refrigerator's temperature. The water bath step also will help cool the base faster, thus there will be less time to wait before the ice cream can be churned (always a plus).

THICKENING THE BASE

When making both a custard-based and a non-custard ice cream, thickening the base is an important step. Most recipes instruct the reader to cook the mixture of milk or cream until it coats the back of a spoon. This means the base should be thick enough to cling to the back of a spoon when you remove it from the base and thick enough to draw and hold a distinguishable line when you draw the spoon through the base.

METRIC VS. WEIGHTS

One of the best tools you can purchase for your kitchen is a scale. Weighing ingredients is inherently more accurate than filling a measuring cup. This is especially true for powdered ingredients such as cocoa powder. Both types of measurements are provided in the cookbook.

AVOIDING ICE CRYSTALS

Ice crystals are the enemy of ice cream. They change the texture of the ice cream from a creamy scoop to a gritty mouthful of unpleasantness. There are a few ways to avoid ice crystals in your ice cream. The first defense is to create a creamy base with minimal water. Thickening the base and reducing moisture from added ingredients, such as fruit, is very important. The second defense is to avoid melting. Do not remove your ice cream from the freezer until you are ready to scoop. Resist the urge to allow your ice cream to melt on the counter before scooping unless absolutely necessary. Each time you let the ice cream melt it must refreeze in the freezer, which creates ice crystals. The third defense is to reduce air exposure. Unless your freezer-safe container is completely filled to the brim with ice cream, press parchment or plastic wrap onto the surface of the ice cream to prevent ice crystals from being able to form. The fourth and final defense against ice crystals is to eat your ice cream. The longer your ice cream sits in the freezer, the more likely it is to melt and refreeze due to the opening and closing of the freezer door. Eating the ice creams in this cookbook should not be too difficult.

CHURNING THE ICE CREAM

If you are new to ice cream making, you may be wondering how long and to what extent to churn your ice cream. The purpose of churning ice cream is to add air to the base, thus producing a creamy, scoopable texture. Churning time partially depends on your ice cream maker. Be sure to thoroughly read the manufacturer's instructions before churning ice cream. Churn until the ice cream base is the consistency of thick soft-serve ice cream. In most machines, the machine will start to sound like it is working a little harder, but this is not guaranteed. When soft-serve consistency is reached and the ice cream begins to pull away from the sides of the canister (because the dasher is no longer scraping ice cream off of the sides of the canister), stop the machine and immediately scoop the ice cream into a freezer-safe container and freeze until firm. If your ice cream falls apart when you scoop it, it was likely over-churned.

STORAGE

Your freezer should be at or below 0°F (-18°C) to best freeze the ice cream canister and store your ice cream. Check the temperature of your freezer with a thermometer to ensure accuracy.

Acknowledgments

First and foremost I would like to thank Page Street Publishing for giving me the opportunity to write this cookbook. It has been a fun and enlightening experience, and I am still pinching myself that my dream of writing a cookbook came true. Thank you in particular to my publisher, Will Kiester, and editor, Marissa Giambelluca, for your ideas and guidance and answering all of my little questions. Thank you to Meg Palmer for introducing Page Street Publishing to Scoop Adventures and sparking this partnership.

Thank you to all of the ice cream shop owners who worked with me and contributed to this project. The cookbook would not have been possible without you. It was exciting to hear the stories of so many shop owners and find other people as passionate about ice cream as me. Best of luck in your current and future ice cream endeavors.

A big thank you to all my recipe testers: Claire Ackerman, Bethany Baker, Hailey Barnes, Francesca Bartha, LeAnne Bird, Sunshine Burgos, Deborah Clendaniel, Jennifer Clendaniel, Sonya Coenen, Ninette Dean, Ryan Dillinger, Sherry Dillinger, Jessica Erfer, Alana Ferrara Hodgson, Auke Jager, Sara Jett, Andy Jou, Anna-Luiza Kontovounissios, Leann Meyers, Irene Oakes, Tobias Oholm, Bekah Powell, Rebecca Rivard-Darby, Heather Russell, Anna Ruzicka, Eric Scheidt, Debbie Shelton, Candace Wafford, Beth Wilkins, Julie Wilkins, and Danielle Young. Your insightful feedback was truly appreciated.

Thank you, Mom and Dad, for being my lifelong cheerleaders. It does not matter what I decide to do or how I decide to do it, you have always been there for me and full of encouraging words. Mom, I also thank you for being my lifelong proofreader. Whether it was my eighth-grade English papers or this cookbook, your words of wisdom have helped me become the writer I am today.

Thank you to all of my friends and family for your never-ending excitement about this project, for your flavor ideas, and for reminding what it is like to make ice cream for the first time. A special thanks to Deborah Clendaniel for your proofreading skills.

Thank you to all my taste testers. There are too many of you to list and you know who you are. Thank you for willingly accepting endless samples and pints of ice cream and providing me with valuable feedback. I know it must have been a tough job *wink.*

Last but not least, I would like to thank my husband, Keith. You have always encouraged me to pursue what I love and not worry about the little things. Thank you for your patience, insight, taste testing, proofreading and hugs when I needed them. I look forward to our future together and hope one day we can enjoy the success of owning our own ice cream shop. I love you.

Participating Ice Cream Businesses

SOUTHEAST

Azucar Ice Cream Company
Miami, Florida
www.azucaricecream.com

Bev's Homemade Ice Cream
Richmond, Virginia
www.facebook.com/
BevsHomemadeIceCream

Dolcezza
Washington, DC
www.dolcezzagelato.com

Ellen's Homemade Ice Cream
Charleston, West Virginia
www.ellensicecream.com

High Road Craft Ice Cream & Sorbet
Atlanta, Georgia
www.highroadcraft.com

Moorenko's
Silver Spring, Maryland
www.moorenkos.com

The Hop Ice Cream Café
Asheville, North Carolina
www.thehopicecreamcafe.com

UDairy Creamery
Newark, Delaware
www.ag.udel.edu/creamery

Wholly Cow Ice Cream
Charleston, South Carolina
www.whollycowicecream.com

SOUTH

Amy's Ice Creams
Austin, Texas
www.amysicecreams.com

Creole Creamery
New Orleans, Louisiana
www.creolecreamery.com

Loblolly Creamery
Little Rock, Arkansas
www.loblollycreamery.com

Mike's Ice Cream
Nashville, Tennessee
www.mikesicecream.com

Roxy's Ice Cream Social
Oklahoma City, Oklahoma
www.roxysicecream.com

Sweet Magnolia Ice Cream Company
Oxford, Mississippi
www.sweetmagnoliaicecream.com

Sam & Greg's
Huntsville, Alabama
www.samandgregs.com

The Comfy Cow
Louisville, Kentucky
www.thecomfycow.com

NORTHEAST

Ample Hills Creamery
Brooklyn, New York
www.amplehills.com

Gerenser's Exotic Ice Cream
New Hope, Pennsylvania
www.gerensersexoticicecream.com

Little Baby's Ice Cream
Philadelphia, Pennsylvania
www.littlebabysicecream.com

lu.lu Ice Cream
Bristol, Vermont
www.luluvt.com

Mount Desert Island Ice Cream
Bar Harbor, Maine
www.mdiic.com

Mystic Drawbridge Ice Cream
Mystic, Connecticut
www.mysticdrawbridgeicecream.com

Sugar & Ice Creamery
Barrington, New Hampshire
www.sugaricecreamery.com

Susanna's Ice Cream and Sorbet
Middleton, Rhode Island
www.sweetberryfarmri.com/
susannasicecream.html

The Bent Spoon
Princeton, New Jersey
www.thebentspoon.net

Toscanini Ice Cream
Cambridge, Massachusetts
www.tosci.com

MIDWEST

Fireflour Pizza
Bismarck, North Dakota
www.fireflourpizza.com

Glacé Artisan Ice Cream
Leawood, Kansas
www.glaceicecream.com

Hartzell's Ice Cream
Bloomington, Indiana
www.hartzellsic.com

Izzy's Ice Cream
Minneapolis, Minnesota
www.izzysicecream.com

Kimmer's Ice Cream
St. Charles, Illinois
www.kimmersicecream.com

Little Brick Ice Cream
Platte, South Dakota
(605) 680-3101

Purple Door Ice Cream
Milwaukee, Wisconsin
www.purpledooricecream.com

Serendipity Homemade Ice Cream
St. Louis, Missouri
www.serendipity-icecream.com

Ted & Wally's
Omaha, Nebraska
www.tedandwallys.com

The Outside Scoop
Indianola, Iowa
(515) 689-1890

Treat Dreams
Ferndale, Michigan
www.treatdreams.com

Young's Jersey Dairy
Yellow Springs, Ohio
www.youngsdairy.com

MOUNTAIN REGION

CloverLeaf Creamery
Buhl, Idaho
www.facebook.com/
CloverLeafCreamery

Dolcetti Gelato
Salt Lake City, Utah
www.dolcettigelato.com

Ice Cream Café
Gillette, Wyoming
(307) 686-8110

Susie Scoops Ice Cream
Incline Village, Nevada
www.susiescoops.com

Sweet Action Ice Cream
Denver, Colorado
www.sweetactionicecream.com

Sweet Peaks Homemade Ice Cream
Whitefish, Montana
www.sweetpeaksicecream.com

Sweet Republic Artisan Ice Cream
Scottsdale, Arizona
www.sweetrepublic.com

Taos Cow Ice Cream Co.
Arroyo Seco, New Mexico
www.taoscow.com

WEST

Dave's Hawaiian Ice Cream
Multiple locations, Oahu, Hawaii
www.daveshawaiianicecream.com

Full Tilt Ice Cream
Seattle, Washington
www.fulltilticecream.com

Hot Licks Homemade Ice Cream
Fairbanks, Alaska
www.hotlicks.net

Mitchell's Ice Cream
San Francisco, California
www.mitchellsicecream.com

Ruby Jewel Ice Cream
Portland, Oregon
www.rubyjewel.net

About the Author

LINDSAY CLENDANIEL is an avid ice cream maker who blogs about her adventures at ScoopAdventures.com. Her blog and recipes have been featured online at the *Huffington Post*, *Redbook Magazine, Gourmet Live* and *Sweet Home*, and the website of the award-winning confectioner Sucré. As a former resident of New Orleans, Lindsay wrote regularly as the New Orleans Dessert Examiner. Lindsay now lives in Annapolis, Maryland, with her husband, two cats and two ice cream makers.

Photo Credits

All photos were taken by Lindsay Clendaniel unless otherwise specified

Action Ice Cream: Page 99 (shop)

Carlos Somoza: Page 27

Danielle Quigley: Page 13

David Bergeron: Page 34

Emily Gilbert: Page 58 (sign)

Eric Wu: Page 64 & 65

Glace Artisan Ice Cream: Page 81 (shop)

Hartzell Martel: Page 89 (shop)

John Young: Page 85 (ice cream)

John Young: Page 85 (sign)

Joshua Cogan: Page 19 (shop)

Keith Clendaniel: Page 183

Kimmer's Ice Cream: Page 77 (owners)

Linda Mitchell: Page 115 (shop)

Luke Bukoski: Page 15 (owners)

Megan Carroll: Page 79

Megan McClure: Page 108 (shop)

Micah Mackenzie: Page 15 (ice cream)

Michael Dedrick: Page 74 (owners)

Mike Perlman: Page 55

Mystic Drawbridge Ice Cream: Page 53 (shop)

Nancy Nolan: Page 31 (shop)

Raena Mutz: Page 40 (truck)

Sugar & Ice Creamery: Page 62

Taos Cow Ice Cream Co.: Page 101

Index